IMPRESSIONIST PAINTINGS
IN THE LOUVRE

IMPRESSIONIST PAINTINGS

IN THE LOUVRE

BY

GERMAIN BAZIN

CONSERVATEUR-EN-CHEF
DU MUSEE DU LOUVRE

LONDON

THAMES AND HUDSON

TRANSLATED FROM THE FRENCH
BY S. CUNLIFFE-OWEN

© THAMES AND HUDSON LONDON 1958
SECOND IMPRESSION (REVISED) 1959
THIRD IMPRESSION (REVISED) 1961
FOURTH IMPRESSION (REVISED) 1963
FIFTH IMPRESSION (REVISED) 1964
SIXTH IMPRESSION 1965
SEVENTH IMPRESSION (REVISED) 1969
EIGHTH IMPRESSION (REVISED) 1972
PRINTED IN GERMANY BY CARL SCHÜNEMANN
REPRODUCTION RIGHTS RESERVED BY S.P.A.D.E.M. PARIS
THIS BOOK IS PUBLISHED IN FRANCE BY
EDITIONS AIMERY SOMOGY PARIS

500 18003 2 CLOTHBOUND
500 20006 8 PAPERBACK

CONTENTS

FOREWORD

IMPRESSIONISM has not yet become part of history. It is still a living legend, with a firmness of purpose which adversity could not destroy, a purity of aim which, perhaps, was only equalled by the pioneers of the Renaissance, and which resulted in complete nonconformity. The boldness of these artists involved them often in tragedy, poverty, sacrifice, opprobrium, but in triumphs as well. This legend has given them the aureole of martyrs. The children of to-day, like the men of yesterday, hearing the story of these lives find it hard to believe.

The heroism of these painters gave their first patrons the feeling that they must continue their apostolate, that their mission in life was to ensure the so often contested triumph of these artists in their own country, and that they had been granted the privilege of binding up their wounds. When Caillebotte gave the signal, the donors swarmed round the gates of the Louvre bringing Impressionist masterpieces with them, three hundred in all, which make our Impressionist gallery the finest in the world, a display, too, due to private enterprise, being State-aided only to the extent of some ten per cent. Here, for the first time, the masterpieces are collected together. Almost a hundred have been chosen for reproduction in colour with a description of their origins and the vicissitudes they underwent. To a greater degree than was the case with the preceding work on the old masters in the Louvre, it has been necessary to go back to the original sources. For Impressionism has only lately acquired its historians. Contemporary testimony, mostly in the shape of memoirs, is not scrupulously exact. Only two of these witnesses, Gustave Geffroy and Tabarant, have left us accurate chronicles. I have had therefore to undertake the most meticulous research for these notes, in which I have been helped by Madame Dreyfus-Bruhl of the Service of Documentation attached to the Picture Department of the Louvre.

The chief purpose of the introduction is to describe the formation of this wonderful museum. The archives of the Louvre, consulted in many cases for the first time, have thrown light on the question of the resistance in official circles to the entry of Impressionist paintings to the National Museums. It will be seen that the curators of museums played a less reprehensible role than a badly informed public opinion has assigned to them.

It seemed to me that the best way of conveying the sense of an 'Impressionist miracle' was to depict the astounding contrast between their martyrdom and their triumph. So as to have a complete understanding of the whole affair, I have tried to show the triumphant success of the Impressionists at the end of the century, both in France and in other countries, and this is preceded by a chapter describing their poverty and distress. For this chapter, I have taken Claude Monet as the heroic example, because of the ample documentation we possess about him. For all these notes we have, in fact, taken care to make use wherever possible only of authentic documents, letters, catalogues, extracts from archives, and have avoided certain celebrated memoirs, which are generally recognised to be largely romanticised.

Nothing shows the vicissitudes undergone by the Impressionists more than the prices their pictures have fetched. From the prices of the pictures acquired since the last war the reader will realise that, before the ridiculous rise in prices of the present day, the Louvre, with only modest means at its disposal, was able to acquire some works of first-class importance.

I have written this book with feelings of gratitude to all those donors who have made this museum possible. Those who deny that the French possess a sense of civic responsibility are advised to visit the Jeu de Paume. This generosity is all the more appreciated, because it is whole hearted and without reservation, for the French government does not allow tax rebate to its benefactors as do the American and British governments. Each donation therefore represents the sacrifice of part of a private patrimony, a sacrifice made for the public good. The Impressionist gallery at the Louvre is not the accomplishment of the French government but of the people of France.

THE BIRTH OF IMPRESSIONISM

IMPRESSIONISM was born from the meeting of two men with names so alike that at first they were often taken for one another: Monet and Manet. From the crossbreeding of their two methods was born modern painting. It would be hard to imagine two more different people. In their social positions they were far apart. Manet was a middle-class Parisian, son of a magistrate, whose horizons were the boulevards, and earth was the pavement. He never accepted the popular verdict that he was a rebel. He made up to the judges at the various Salons, and managed in the end to get hold of the Legion of Honour, at a time when his comrades in the fight were still being treated as pariahs. After the Commune, in 1870, had burnt part of Paris, Manet was held in horror as a rebel and insurgent, and all that was revolutionary in art and literature was laid at his door. The disapproval of society changed this gentle-mannered person into an exasperated being.

Monet, on the other hand, did not worry about being unpopular. In opinions he inclined to the Left, though he never went in actively for politics like Pissarro. He therefore felt no need of a middle-class audience whose support was so vital to Manet. What exasperated him (and not Manet who was well off) were the dreary problems of how to live. He was a man of the people. In his old age they called him the 'old man of Giverny'. The world of conventions which paralyses the bourgeois meant nothing to Monet. Poor and without resources he had to create everything, himself first of all. He did not fail, and followed the straight line of his destiny, while Manet, after 1870, made repeated attempts to please the judges. Monet had the frankness of an open-air man. Beside that sea which was the background picture to his whole life, he breathed in the great winds from childhood onwards, and often gazed at its restless waves which were for him a symbol of the infinite.

Nothing could have seemed less likely than that these two painters should have belonged to the same school. Their attitudes towards the problem of the relations between art and nature, which was the great debate of the century, were totally different. Manet was blind to the world. Monet had eyes for nothing else.

EDGAR DEGAS *Portrait of Manet and his wife* (detail)

THOMAS COUTURE *Self-portrait*

Both men, however, formed their style by 'copying': Monet the beaches of Ste-Adresse, and Manet pictures in the museums. The Louvre was the great art school of the century. Hitherto, the artist had been the pupil of a master; henceforth he was the pupil of the old masters. All, or almost all, from Delacroix and Théodore Rousseau to Courbet, Degas, Renoir, and Matisse, formed their style by copying the old masterpieces in the Louvre which they found especially suited their own temperament.

Manet was no exception. Rejected by Couture who told him, 'You will never be more than the Daumier of your epoch', he made for the Louvre, taking his paints with him. Perhaps with Manet, alternately condemned and praised for being a 'museum painter', the formative effect of the old masters is more apparent than in the case of the others. Delacroix, Courbet, Degas,

11

Renoir only used these pictures as exercises in painting and copied them exactly. They rarely borrowed from them themes for their own pictures. The example of *Parisian Women dressed as Algerians,* obviously inspired by the *Women of Algiers* by Delacroix, would be unique but for Manet.

When in 1908 Professor Gustave Pauli wrote an article maintaining that the *Picnic* (page 114) by Manet was inspired purely and simply by an engraving after Raphael, it was supposed that Manet was trying to mystify the judges of the Salon. Perhaps such a notion was not altogether absent from his thoughts and certainly the procedure of borrowing a whole composition was a regular proceeding with Manet, even when he had reached the fullness of his powers. This need, always to base his art on the work of an old master, did not escape his contemporaries. Courbet said of Manet, 'This young fellow must not merely give us pictures à la Velasquez.' The most cutting remark of all was made by Alfred Stevens, a friend of Manet, when he said that 'the engraver Bellot', a personage in the *Bon Bock,* 'was drinking pure beer from Haarlem'.

Why did Manet not himself invent his subjects and his compositions? Because those particular problems did not interest him.

Manet's imagination was unable to suggest a theme around which could be built up a composition or an action. His mind abhorred fiction. The subject was for him only an excuse to paint, the choice of one a matter of indifference, except in so far as it was as empty of moral intention as possible, and served his wishes as an artist. Therefore he trusted opportunity to bring him ready-made subjects (Café scenes, the *Execution of Maximilian, View of the Rue de Berne,* during the day of the Fête Nationale on the occasion of the Universal Exhibition, the *Fight between the Kersage and the Alabama*), opportunity, and also tradition.

Apart from Delacroix and Corot, one the heir of the Baroque tradition and the other of the classical, and Géricault, a stand-in for Michelangelo, all nineteenth-century painters suffered from composition-crisis. In this crisis, Courbet rejoined Ingres, and even David, recopying antique basreliefs, thus early showed the tendency. Nearly all artists of the nineteenth century are portrait painters, either of Man or Nature. When they have to compose, they juxtapose their portraits: Courbet, painting the *Burial at Ornans,* proceeded in exactly the same way as David painting the *Coronation.*

This neglect of composition, due to an ever keener wish to exploit direct

PABLO PICASSO *Portrait of Elie Faure*

feeling, resulted in a complete absence of composition in Monet's *Water-lilies,* and in a supremely realistic slice of life, together with a masterly glimpse of the world beyond appearances, in the work of Degas.

For Manet, the problem of painting did not lie in formal arrangement, nor even in the discovery of an original form, and even less in the expression of moral issues. Manet to some extent liquidated the Romantics. He rid painting of all moral and intellectual preoccupations, and boldly and frankly, so that, in the words of Elie Faure, he became the 'primitive of a new age', restored it to itself. He brought back, after so much storm and stress, the pure pleasure of that painting for its own sake, discovered by Frans Hals and Velasquez, which consists in manipulating dabs of colour, and not bothering about anything else, so as to transcribe the fairy-like

13

AUGUSTE RENOIR *Alfred Sisley and his wife*

beauty of the various visual aspects of the world.

Manet's art is in fact purely a problem of colour, and not a problem of light as with Monet. Composition, involving mental exercise, embarrasses this painter, for whom painting lies beyond all mental processes. He uses the most elementary methods. We find with him, systematically, composition by juxtaposition. Sometimes he tries, not to compose, but to let his picture 'flow'. Sometimes again he gets rid of this worry altogether by simply borrowing wholesale a composition of some well-known master, or again he collects into a single canvas several different fragments taken from different pictures, as in *Fishing*, usually being careful to invert the borrowed forms doubtless to put researchers off the track.

Does this imitativeness diminish Manet's originality as a creative artist? It raises once more the old problem of imitation in art, but only in the second degree. It is no longer a question of whether the artist should imitate natural forms, but if he has the right to imitate forms created before him by other painters. The answer lies in the pictures themselves. We have not exhausted the 'modernity' of the *Picnic*, plagiarised from Raphael, and as for *Olympia*, inspired by the *Venus of Urbino*, it is still, to-day, just as 'Baudelairian'.

While Manet, chased off the premises by Couture, went to seek his salvation in the Louvre, Monet left Gleyre's studio in 1863, and took Renoir and Sisley with him to paint in the forest of Fontainebleau, a haunt of artists 'with the Nature-worship malady' since the eighteenth century. Manet had prepared the way. He destroyed in one fell swoop the literary taint in pictures, at a time, not so different from our own, when painting and literature were embedded in one another. Manet led the painters back to their palettes, and Monet taught them to use their eyes. Dangerous though it is to make comparisons over so long an interval of time, and with such differences of style, I would hazard that in this birth of modern painting, Manet's position is that of a Romanesque artist, while Monet's attitude is Gothic.

The Romanesque sculptor inherited a vast vocabulary of shapes and images going back to the beginnings of civilisation. He invented within a

CLAUDE MONET *The cathedral of Rouen*

tradition, using his stock to the full, finding in new associations of ancient elements the forgotten meaning of these rhythms and forms. The Romanesque imagist thus rediscovered sculpture just as Manet rediscovered painting. The Gothic artist escapes from all this world which haunts the imagination of the Romanesque artist, and with joyful vigour, reminding one of Impressionism, he invents a style originating in nature itself. The gesture which Descartes later called 'the clean sweep' is an essential factor in the French make-up, which always has to return, after many detours, to the basic principle of observed facts. Thus, Impressionism and Gothic art are the most precious contributions of France to Western art. It is surely not mere chance which caused Impressionism and the Gothic to meet with Monet at Rouen, Sisley at Moret, and Pissarro at Dieppe.

For a century painters had been tentatively looking for something which Monet was the first to find ... the art of seeing. Other artists always looked through a screen of antecedent art forms: Corot through Poussin and Claude, Théodore Rousseau through Ruisdael and Hobbema. To see properly is the hardest thing. It requires genius. Most people see by way of their parents, their masters, or the social milieu in which they live. Sometimes on a youthful morning the scales fall from their eyes and the world appears, but only for a second, and for the rest of their lives they only look through that sombre curtain of images at the universe situated beyond. Only painters and poets really see. Braque, full of this prophetic role of the painter, said to me one day, 'It was Monet who invented sea bathing'. It existed before him, made fashionable by the Duchesse de Berry who used to bathe at Dieppe, and one can go back farther. At the end of the eighteenth century, the Benedictines of Catania in Sicily, who were sybaritically inclined, had their bathing cabins on the beach. But Braque was right. Though Monet did not invent sea bathing, he and Boudin were the first to 'see' it. Man often needs a generation to 'see' something which he has himself created. The act of looking tends to follow after the act of thinking; only a few prophets of genius are able to look first.

Behold then Monet in the forest of Fontainebleau, the least likely locale to be the cradle of Impressionism. Oudry, in Louis XV's reign, was the first to go there in order to get the background for his hunting pictures. By the end of the eighteenth century a few painters, such as Bruandet, still went there. After 1830, both the Romantics (Th. Rousseau, Diaz, Millet) and the Neo-Classical school (Corot, D'Aligny, Bertin) frequented it and it became a kind of landscape Academy. Like his predecessors, Monet made for the high woods. They, however, went to find shade while he went to find light. He returned several times up to 1870, staying at an inn at Chailly-en-Bière. There he started out upon probably the boldest pictorial enterprise of the century. Its importance, owing to the misfortunes which befell him, passed practically unnoticed by the critics, until a recent gift to the Louvre drew attention once more to this masterpiece, alas mutilated.

A canvas some thirty-three square yards in area, larger therefore than Courbet's *Studio*, was the proposition which, against all reason, this young man of twenty-five, and penniless, who had only painted a few landscape sketches and some still-lifes, intended to carry out. It was to show some ten persons, met together in the freshness of the green wood for a picnic. Monet intended to show this gigantic work in the Salon of 1866. We do not know why he could not offer it, probably because it was not his to dispose of, having been left with the innkeeper as surety. He replaced it by an open-air portrait of Camille, his mistress. As to the big picture, he recovered it, ruined by damp, from the innkeeper's cellar, and cut out the central group, now in a Paris collection. The left-hand part has recently been given to the Louvre; a sketch in the Moscow Museum records the composition as a whole.

Passages in letters from Monet to Bazille, and allusions in Boudin's letters, bear witness to the importance Monet attached to this picture for which he made Bazille and Camille pose. In April he summoned Bazille and confessed that 'the prospect scared him'; to his friend who had not yet come to pose he wrote on May 4: 'Don't leave me in the lurch. I think of nothing but my picture and if I had to give it up I think I should go mad.' On August 16 he again summoned Bazille. 'I am in despair. I'm afraid you're going to make me spoil my picture.' He underwent many vicissitudes for in the summer of 1865 he broke his leg. Because of its huge size the work was not painted outside, but at the inn after sketches done in the open air. Monet's friends regarded the whole thing as fantasy. Boudin, who had given Monet the subject, considered he had gone too far. In a letter of 1865, he speaks of 'this huge sandwich which costs the earth'. As for the always traditional Manet, he said of Monet in 1866: 'Just look at that young fellow trying to paint out of doors; as if the old masters had ever done such a thing!' Courbet was more understanding. During the spring of 1866, he was at Chailly advising Monet who was hurrying to finish his picture for the

Salon, pointing out several things to be altered. These differences can be seen by comparison with the sketch in the Moscow Museum and also by the X-ray photos of the fragment in the Louvre.

What had Monet in view when painting this colossal picture? Doubtless he wanted to demonstrate that a scene of to-day can also be worthy of a large format. He was following Manet's example in *his* painting, but going beyond the bounds which the latter had set in his work of more modest dimensions, painted in the studio and 'underpinned' by Raphael. He hoped to be the real 'modern painter', whom Baudelaire had summoned to show 'how fine and beautiful we are in our ties and patent-leather boots'. Hélène Adhémar has noted that the *Picnic* immediately followed the publication of Baudelaire's study of Constantin Guys (November 1863—April 1864) in which he aired his views on modernism. The young artist must have met the poet at Commandant Lejosne's, who was a relation of Bazille's, during the winter of 1864/65, which preceded work on the *Picnic*. Surely, the young women in the *Picnic* are Constantin Guys', let loose upon Nature. As for the huge size, this was evidently due to the wish to rival Courbet. Bigness is, in any case, an obsession with all the nineteenth-century paint-ers, starting with the giant productions of David and Gros. Their size made the Salon public look at them, and proved to the judges the ability of the artist to compose. To succeed at the Salon was the aim of every artist, because it was the only selling medium.

This picture is a study of light on an enormous scale. Monet noticed the pools of colour with which the light, filtering through the leaves, splashed the clothing and the faces; but he also noticed an effect contrary to the teaching in the schools, namely that light does not dim but intensifies colour, rescues it from the shadow. Colour, therefore, when submitted to the play of light and shade, tends to break up. This fragmentation is conveyed in the study in the Moscow Museum, which is treated as a sketch, as with all the studies he painted at that time, by hatching with rapid brush strokes. In the big picture, Monet worked in the manner of Courbet, with strong slabs of colour which he considered better suited to the monumental scale of the work.

We have to-day to reconstruct this mighty work with the aid of our imagination. The sketches and fragments which have been preserved attest its beauty. The still-life lighted by a patch of sunshine in the centre portion is splendid. But it is the piece preserved in the Louvre which alone conveys

CLAUDE MONET *Portrait of Madame Gaudibert*

the atmosphere which Monet was trying to achieve, that poetry of a sunlit glade on a summer's day. One is staggered by the audacity of those enormous lumps of cobalt by means of which the sky literally pierces the foliage. The composition is delightfully easy. Whereas Manet could only conceive a picture by copying an old theme, Monet excelled in bringing together his numerous personages quite naturally, a problem by no means easy owing to the lack of action. The tree trunk on the right and Bazille's long legs provide the horizontal and vertical coordinates of the pictures. The centre holds the brightest light, the still-life, thrown into relief by the shade of the thick forest; towards this centre, all the figures converge.

There is no doubt that Monet's purpose before 1870 was to paint Man, life size, in his natural surroundings. In no way discouraged by the failure of his *Picnic,* he painted, on a smaller scale, but still exceptionally

19

AUGUSTE RENOIR *Portrait of Claude Monet*

large, his *Women in the Garden* (page 151) which he began in the same year in which he finished   the *Picnic* (1866). This time the picture was painted out of doors, necessitating a trench and a pulley. The method is no longer the monumental one of the *Picnic*, but rather the rapid, 'throw-away' technique of the sketches for it. *Women in the Garden* was refused by the Salon of 1867. Monet, rebuffed, never again produced an open-air composition of this magnitude. After *The Green Dress* (or *Camille*) which replaced the *Picnic* at the last moment in the Salon of 1866, he produced one more lifesize figure, *Madame Gaudibert,* which was painted in the same year as the *Women in the Garden*. Renoir followed Monet's example (*Lise,* Salon of 1868) and never gave up painting the human figure. Bazille remembered the *Picnic* for which he had posed when, in 1867, he painted the *Family Reunion* (page 110). Monet's last large human figure was *Camille in Japanese Dress,* painted in 1876. Except for this picture, Monet, after 1870, abandoned his ambitious designs of placing modern man in his full stature in natural surroundings, and restricted himself to studying problems of light and colour. The painter who, at an age when others were taking their first steps, had conceived this bold and powerful idea, reduced his art by ever more exact and finer analysis to ever more subtle expressions of visual phenomena. The man who had produced a colossus, of his own free will henceforth only painted fragments. Monet's initiative did, however, show results in Renoir, who between 1875 and 1881 produced several

Claude Monet in his garden

works, three of which are in the Louvre (pages 178, 180, 181). These are the direct result of Monet's *Picnic* (page 148). They are studies of the effect of light filtered through foliage on to people coming and going in these warm, throbbing shadows. The *Moulin de la Galette* is the most Impressionist, the most vital, of these pictures. But Monet's grand design reached its end in Renoir's *The Boating Party* (Phillips Collection, Washington) painted in 1881. It stands at the end of what one may call, in Impressionism, the 'Cycle of Picnics'. These modern artists were seduced by this theme, for it enabled them to paint an organic composition, based on a natural agreement of gesture and expression resulting from the intimate atmosphere produced by a meal eaten together, on a summer Sunday, far from the cares of every day, happy in the light of the fine weather, light which comes sifting down through leaves or awnings, bringing the blood back to the cheeks of the girls, and the light of desire to the eyes of the men. The mystery religions of the last days of the ancient world, and even the Christian religion itself, have exploited this atmosphere derived from the union of souls, created by *agapē*, and Plato places his deepest reflections in the setting of a banquet. For an instant of time, the quirks of individuality cease to annoy, the worst enmities calm down, and all the human beings round that table become but one being and one soul. Each seems to live only for the others, but on the borders of the *agapē* is Eros, and at any moment, beneath the sign of love, what was meant as a gift is taken by force. The theme of the picnic is, in fact, another version of the older *Concert Champêtre*. Music was then the uniter of souls and the agent of Eros, aided and abetted by Nature. Manet was well aware of this, for he admitted to Antonin Proust that he had in mind Giorgione's *Concert Champêtre*, which he had copied in the Louvre when he was young.

The theme of the picnic was traditional in French art. When it was given up by the Classicists and Romantics alike, painting became escapist, retiring into history and quitting contemporary life. In the seventeenth century, a meal taken in common, bringing together the peasant and his family and sometimes the master and the farmer, was one of the favourite subjects of Le Nain. In the eighteenth century, whether it was oysters or ham, the meal was a subject for gallantry, and generally formed part of what one may call the 'Cycle of the Hunt'. There are even picnics. It is not surprising that, in a country where cooking is one of the fine arts, this theme should have often inspired artists. But the frequency of meals in

22

HENRI FANTIN-LATOUR *The atelier des Batignolles*

EDOUARD MANET *Portrait of Berthe Morisot*

Impressionist art is a way of expressing the sociability of Impressionism. No school of painting has ever taken so much trouble to describe the life of its contemporaries, to show them their own pleasures, to help them forget their sorrows. No school of painting was ever so optimistic. By inaugurating the theme of the picnic in modern painting, Manet showed himself to be, in some respects, a primitive. (In 1858, in a small picture, Pissarro had painted a picnic by the roadside at Montmorency, but the subject was a mere anecdote.) The personages posing in a Batignolles studio, in front of a natural décor borrowed from the theatre, do not communicate with one another. One asks indeed in what way the obligation to take up the attitude of a river god could make the man in the toque feel natural. In his entry to the Salon of 1869, entitled *Luncheon in the Studio* or *After the Coffee* (Munich Museum), Manet puts no more life than he puts into his *Picnic*. This picture is hardly more than a posed portrait of Léon Koella-Leenhoff in front of a splendid still-life, with the figure of a servant in the background to set him off. The conversation at the tête-à-tête meal, *Chez le Père Lathuile* (1879), is more lively. Manet, who had followed Monet's example and begun to paint out of doors, made an effort to be more natural. Nevertheless the people in the picture are still obviously posing.

It is this naturalness which gives its gay charm to Monet's *Picnic* (page 178). The light gracefulness of his women with their dresses brushing the leaves is very moving. On this lovely summer's day, they loved and laughed and lived and now all that is left of them are their passing shapes in a picture. Such human emotions never result from looking at Manet's work (except when he painted Berthe Morisot), because his people only belonged to the studio. Monet chose the moment before the picnic starts. The varied movements and gestures of the people settling themselves round the tablecloth, on to which the food has been unpacked, provide the action. The faces, however, remain rather impersonal, perhaps because Monet only had two models for all of them, Bazille and Camille, and it is by their attitudes, their outlines, and above all by the harmonious way in which all the elements have been brought together, that the people in the composition are alive. Quite soon after the Chailly-en-Bière picture. Monet returned to the idea of a meal, but this time indoors. These pictures were painted in 1868 at Fécamp, when Monet was temporarily at peace owing to the support of Monsieur Gaudibert. With his mistress and his young son he began to know something of family happiness, a respite in a harassing poverty-stricken existence. He has made the meal a symbol of happiness. Camille and little Jean are sitting round a table and are beginning their meal. On the floor lies the humble cardboard doll of this child of poverty. A maid is disappearing, her profile barely visible; a woman wearing a hat and veil, a visitor, is leaning out of the window. In 1868, also, Monet painted a dinner by lamplight, which tradition says was at Sisley's house, but the little boy is once more present at table, at which are also sitting a man and two women. Finally another picture shows the same table bare, the same absence of tension; the woman is sewing, while the man, leaning on the chimney-piece, is talking to her, in the quiet moment when dinner is over.

In Renoir's *Fin du Déjeuner*, in the Staedel Institute at Frankfurt-am-Main, where the scene is a café, and where the man is lighting a cigarette, the carnations worn by the two women, whom the meal has brightened up, gleam in hot shadows with their peach-like texture. *The Boating Party*, painted two years later, is a bigger affair altogether. Fourteen people take part. Napkins are lying on the table which is in disorder, several guests have already got up; some are sneezing, some are flirting; laughter mixes with the general cheerfulness; a group of men are talking apart; a girl playing with her dog makes a face at the pekinese; the women are in summer frocks and the men, who have spent the morning canoeing, are wearing flannel waistcoats and straw hats. A big step has been taken since Monet's guests went picnicking in crinolines and the men did not dare appear even in shirtsleeves!

The Boating Party has also been mutilated, though not to the same extent as Monet's *Picnic*. It has none the less altered the appearance of this striking work. It was until quite recently one of the best preserved of Renoir's canvases, and in better condition than the *Moulin de la Galette* where the change in the colours, deplored by Renoir at the end of his life, has unfortunately softened the lake colours and made blue the dominant hue of the picture. Renoir, having noticed, about 1880, this change in tone, took precautions to avoid it, which is why *The Boating Party* was in fine condition only a few years ago, when I saw it in Washington. Alas, since then, the hand of a restorer has caused the almost imperceptible gradations in transparence, which produced both the fruit-like quality of the flesh and the symphonic modulation of the toning, to disappear, with the result that we now have a hard picture with brutish models wearing fixed expressions.

26

The subtle link joining all these personages has vanished. Parisian art-lovers scarcely recognised the picture when it was on view at the Orangery in 1955 among the 'Masterpieces in American Collections'.

After 1870, there was a break in Monet's work. The man who had dreamed of huge compositions painted from now on only easel pictures of pure landscape, the figures being themselves part of the landscape, and it was only at the end of his life that, haunted once more by the idea of size, he painted some huge water-lilies. This new attempt at painting on a

AUGUSTE RENOIR *Monet painting in his garden*

monumental scale was inspired by very different ideas from those which had inspired the *Picnic;* Man who was the centre of the latter picture was eliminated. Carried away by some kind of cosmic dream to become absorbed in the universal, Monet abandoned all composition.

Impressionism would therefore probably have run a different course but for the misfortunes attending Monet's *Picnic.* The rejection of figures and of composition would perhaps not have occurred and the reaction against pure Impressionism which occurred after 1895 with Seurat and Gauguin would have found less justification.

It was only poverty and the inability to get accepted by the Salon which caused Monet's courageous and noble enterprise to founder. This refusal to artists of their right to show their work compelled the innovators to get together and form a group. But a picture gallery is not the Salon. One does not paint for the Rue le Peletier or the Rue Lafitte, in the same way as one would for the vast spaces of the official exhibition. Also one must live and to live one must produce work for the art lover, who does not want huge pictures. Our painters were therefore discouraged from large-scale compositions like those which the great masters of old had painted and which are no longer possible except on official commission. They have to work to a small scale on their easels. Thus, one of the major works of French painting, which might have been the 'picture of the century', vanished into oblivion.

POVERTY AND GENIUS

PAINTERS to-day do not take the risk that history will forget them. Before they have finished their life they make sure of a biographer. Their story begins to be given to the public on the occasion of their first show. The masters of 1910 were surrounded with witnesses who early on pinned down all the circumstances of their lives; the argus eye of the Press was upon them and published the result, which they preserved in their press-cutting albums. I flatter myself that I, too, indicated to the critics this historic sense of the present when, in 1933/34, with René Huyghe, I undertook a study of the painters of to-day as if they had lived two centuries ago; it was at that time that I wrote the greater part of those 400 bibliographical notices devoted to the painters of all nations, which form the first dictionary of contemporary art.

In the case of the Impressionists, things were very different. What we know about them has been told us, in the form of memories, by their friends. Thirty years after their deaths, when the artists were famous, they told us what they could remember of the days of struggle. This has resulted in many contradictions and uncertainties. Our only accurate information comes from their correspondence, fortunately copious, but much of which still remains unpublished. Monet's letters to Bazille, for example, so valuable for the history of the beginnings of the movement, are only known to us in extracts. We have to guess at a great deal, for we seldom possess both the letter and the answer to it.

It is not easy to discover how these young people lived before 1870, without art-loving patrons and with no galleries such as are available for shows to the young painters to-day. The problem does not arise in the case of Manet, Bazille, Sisley, Degas, and Berthe Morisot, who were of middle-class parentage and had enough money to devote themselves to their art. The same goes for Cézanne. The modest allowance of 200 francs per month given him by his father (reduced to 100 when his father got to hear of his liaison with Hortense Fiquet) was enough for a frugal existence. He also had a few other sources of income, and had his keep paid at Aix. Those who had to fight against hunger and destitution were Renoir,

EDGAR DEGAS *Self-portrait in a soft hat*   AUGUSTE RENOIR *Self-portrait*

Pissarro, and Monet. We know little about Renoir's difficulties. In any case he had a gay and optimistic nature, and faced adversity with good humour. It was not so with Monet who never accepted poverty and gives vent to a kind of fury against fate in his begging letters. Thanks to numerous letters in which he lets his friends know all about his lamentable condition, we can see that life, for all these painters, until after their fiftieth year, was an unending drama. It needed heroic courage not to give up, not to make concessions in order to please the public and find buyers.

The one we know least about before 1870 is Pissarro. When he arrived in Paris from the West Indies in 1852, having fled the family business, his father made him an allowance, but we do not know for how long. His friend Ludovic Piette probably helped him occasionally. Ten years later Pissarro married and had seven children, the first of whom was born on February 20, 1863, and the last on August 22, 1884. The worries of bringing up a family were increased by the fact that all his sons were

30

painters and confronted him during their youth with the same difficulties he had known in his own. In 1878 he explained how he started, as follows: 'I was at St. Thomas in the West Indies in 1852, a well-paid clerk, but chucked everything and fled to Caracas, Venezuela, so as to sever my links with middle-class life. That I suffered horribly is obvious, but I stayed alive. My sufferings at this moment are even worse, much worse, than when I was young and enthusiastic. I am certain there is no future for me. All the same, I would not hesitate to do it all over again.'

Renoir, fifth child of a poor tailor in Limoges, was apprenticed to a porcelain manufacturer at fourteen. Working at various decorative tasks, he had succeeded by the age of twenty-one in putting by enough money to enrol at the Ecole des Beaux-Arts. In 1862 he joined Gleyre's classes. How long did these savings last? We do not know. But we hear of Renoir picking up discarded tubes of paint, thrown away by his comrades at Gleyre's studio. Diaz certainly came to his help by opening an account for him at the shop where he bought his materials. Later on Bazille looked after him. In 1867 he was living in the latter's studio in the Rue de Furstenberg and sharing his meals. All the same we do not know what expedients he used to live up till 1870.

Monet, before painting landscapes in the open air on Boudin's advice, had made some money at Le Havre by drawing caricatures which had a great success. He gave this money to his aunt Lecadre who doled it out to him for his needs. His father allowed him to go to Paris for a few months in 1859. Encouraged by Troyon, Monet prolonged his stay. Unfortunately his refusal to enrol at the Beaux-Arts caused his father to stop his allowance, and he had to have recourse to the pittance left at Aunt Lecadre's. Later on he lived at Government expense, because he did his military service in Algeria, his family having refused to buy him off. He was taken ill in Algeria and returned to Le Havre in 1862 to recuperate. When his sick leave was up, his family took pity on him and now *did* buy him out of the army. A civilian once more he began to paint at Le Havre, strongly influenced by Jongkind. Aunt Lecadre followed his work with interest, but did not understand it, so she told Armand Gautier. She complained that he never knew how to finish a picture and that 'he always found some fool to congratulate him': Jongkind and Boudin doubtless! It was thought that life in Paris would suit him better and his father sent him there with a recommendation to the artist Toulmouche, a genre painter, who had just married one of his cousins. In November 1862 Monet was in Paris attending Gleyre's classes. He continued to go there to please his family and ensure the continuation of his allowance. But at the beginning of 1864, Gleyre, threatened with blindness, closed his studio. In the summer Monet rejoined his family at Le Havre and Ste-Adresse. Bazille joined him there at one time and wrote to his father: 'I have lunched with Monet's family. They are charming people and have a delightful property at Ste-Adresse near Le Havre. I had to refuse their kind invitation to spend August with them.' However, the family were beginning to consider their son Claude a good for nothing. There were quarrels and Monet was asked to leave. He went back to Paris at the end of 1864.

Then something pleasant happened. The hanging committee of the 1864 Salon, fearing a new Salon des Refusés as in the previous year, showed more latitude; it welcomed Manet's *Olympia* and two views of Honfleur by Monet. These were successful right away. Critics praised them, and painters wrote to Monet. This success produced a *volte-face* in the attitude of his family. Monet took advantage of it in the following year by embarking on the mad enterprise of the *Picnic*. His friends were concerned to see him at grips with the colossus, 'which was costing him the eyes out of his head'. It was then that the series of catastrophes began. Monet painted his colossal picture in an inn at Chailly-en-Bière. He was charged for his board there over several months not more than 2 francs 50 to 3 francs per day. But he could not pay, so left the picture with the innkeeper as surety, and when he was able to redeem it—he does not tell us when that was— the damp had spoilt part of it and he determined to cut it up.

Doubtless his exasperated family had cut off his allowance. It was temporarily restored in 1866 after the success he had at the Salon with his *Camille* or *The Green Dress*. One sees the importance the Salon had for these young painters. It was their only medium through which to make themselves known and sell their work. Marcellin Desboutins tells in a letter how the stupidity of the judges caused him to lose all the benefits of being launched at the Salon which he had carefully arranged for beforehand with the critics. For Monet, the success of *Camille* at the 1866 Salon meant that Arsène Houssaye bought it.

The family did not continue the allowance for very long. It was Bazille who became Monet's source of supply. In the autumn of 1866, to escape from his creditors, Monet fled to Le Havre, taking with him his big

canvas *Women in the Garden*. Hoping to prevent the forced sale of the two hundred pictures he had left behind at Ville d'Avray, he mutilated them. They were none the less sold at thirty francs for fifty. At Le Havre, the situation was such that he had to destroy earlier canvases to use again, by scraping off the paint, and in December 1866 he wrote to Bazille to send him for this purpose the canvases which he had left behind in various places in Paris and which he carefully describes, thus giving us considerable regret for something we shall never see. We do not know if these canvases were really recovered. On December 1, Monet renewed his request to Bazille, then on the 22nd, as the latter had not replied, he made the same request to Zacharie Astruc. It would be interesting to use X-rays on the pictures painted at Le Havre and Honfleur at this time. The laboratories might reveal traces of drama. Bazille did, however, do all he could to help his friend. He bought *Women in the Garden* for 2,500 francs, which he paid by instalments of 50 francs a month. He persuaded his friend Commandant Lejosne to give 200 francs for a still-life. Monet had also some patrons here and there and a few commissions, as his letters to Bazille reveal.

But his situation deteriorated. The Committee of 1867 refused the *Women in the Garden*. Thinking to soften his father's heart, he revealed the existence and pregnancy of Camille, his mistress. Bazille, sheltering the artist in his studio, wrote to Monet's father in an attempt to mitigate his severity. We have the lesson in middle-class respectability which came in reply. Conditions are laid down. Monet is to stay with his Aunt Lecadre at Ste-Adresse and abandon his mistress. As Aunt Lecadre needs quiet, Monet must cease his escapades and give proof of 'good conduct'. The poor artist, being penniless, had no option but to obey these conditions. He left for Ste-Adresse, leaving alone in Paris, without money, Camille, whom he entrusted to the care of a doctor of one of his friends. In June and July and August he was bothering Bazille, who was in the South of France, for money. In July he received 50 francs which he at once sent to Camille. His parents having refused him everything but his keep, he could not go to Paris for the birth of his son Jean. He had to borrow money from other people and suffer humiliation. He wrote to Bazille, 'Camille gave birth to a fine big boy whom, despite everything, I can't help feeling fond of and I suffer from knowing that his mother has not enough to eat. Neither she nor I have a penny'. In despair, he ended by overwhelming his friend with reproaches and, exasperated by the latter's continued silence, even was so ill mannered as to write to Bazille's father. However, the two artists never quarrelled, and Bazille was Jean's godfather.

To crown everything, Monet had eye trouble that summer, and found it difficult to paint out of doors. He arrived in Paris in the autumn and stayed with Bazille. 'Monet dropped from the skies on me with a collection of magnificent pictures', wrote Bazille to his sisters. 'I am now lodging two impecunious artists, for Renoir is also here. It's like a nursing home. I love it. I have enough room for myself and they are both extremely cheerful.'

Although on the best terms with his family, who were moneyed folk and approved of his wish to be a painter, Bazille, obliged to lend everyone money, had himself sometimes to appeal to his father for help. One day he asked for 'one hundred little francs' to pay a model. The family wanted to get him married. The correspondence shows him putting aside matri-

monial plans with irony and cynicism. 'This idea of marriage was very far
from my thoughts some time back, but now it gets hold of me from time
to time. All the same I find it horrible to tie myself up with a girl (however well bred and musical, which is the formula) who looks down from her
window trying to make up her mind which of the fellows lined up below
pleases her most.' And in another letter, 'I tell myself that one doesn't find a
fortune in the roadway. I almost want to find out what it all adds up to. To
look costs nothing. I feel violent love for no one. But I would not be sorry
to offer a lock of my hair to my future intended, and if they continue to

FRÉDÉRIC BAZILLE *The artist's studio*

fall out as at present, in three years time that will be impossible.' But Bazille remained like Corot a bachelor to devote himself to painting.

Certainly he had the advantage over his friends of being sheltered from want, but their bohemianism and their affairs of the heart ended by making him hard up. One day he even had to pawn his watch. At the beginning of 1868 Monet was once more penniless, and sent, disguised as good wishes for the New Year, a horrible and insulting letter to Bazille on January 1, in which he wrote down all the details of his household expenditure and claimed as a right what Bazille had done for him out of the goodness of his heart, that the latter should pay for the lot. Poverty must have hit Monet really hard to reduce him to such unfairness and unpleasantness.

Bazille's first offended gesture was to reply in the same vein. Gaston Poulain has found in his papers the draft of an answer to Monet in which Bazille, too, made up his accounts. But his own fortunate situation rendered him indulgent towards the excesses of language forced on his friends by poverty and he never sent his cruel letter. He did not, however, in all probability, reply quite in his usual manner, for Monet's exasperation only increased.

In the spring of 1868, Boudin succeeded in getting Manet, Courbet and Monet invited to send work to an International Maritime Exhibition at Le Havre. Monet's success on this occasion won him a silver medal and made him known in his native town, where a shipowner, Monsieur Gaudibert, commissioned a portrait of his wife. In addition to this, Arsène Houssaye, Inspector of Fine Arts and a director of the *Artiste*, bought *Camille* for the then considerable sum of 800 francs.

But now a new misfortune befell Monet. From Paris, on April 26, Boudin wrote to his dealer, Martin, 'Do you know that Monet has come back from Etretat very hungry and depressed? It appears that when your exhibition closed, all his canvases were seized and sold for the benefit of his opponents. Gaudibert got the big seascapes for the miserable sum of 80 francs, I think. Monet still maintains that his aunt is severe with him and keeps back his weekly allowance.'

At the beginning of the summer, Monet went to stay at Fécamp with Camille and Jean, but was once again asked to leave the inn and was homeless. On June 28, 1868, he wrote distractedly to Bazille: 'I write these few words in haste to ask you to help me quickly. I was certainly born under an unlucky star. They have just thrown me out of the inn, naked as a worm. I've found shelter for Camille and my poor little Jean for a few days in the neighbourhood. I'm off to Le Havre this evening to see if I can't get something out of my shipowner. My family won't do anything for me any more. I don't know where I shall sleep to-morrow night.' The postscript reveals an act of despair, which Monet's family denied, many years later, had taken place, but which cannot be ignored, for Monet cannot be suspected of having used quite such a despicable method of extorting money as to have invented it. 'P.S. I was so upset yesterday that I did a very stupid thing and threw myself into the water, happily with no ill effects.' One shudders to think what this suicide, if it had come off, would have cost the world in masterpieces. In May, June, and July, Monet continued to badger Bazille, who repeatedly obliged, sending him 50 francs in May, June, and July, 100 in August, and two sums of 60 in September. In August, Monet showed impatience: 'The baby is ill at the hotel and we haven't a penny.' In September his patron at Le Havre, Monsieur Gaudibert, asked Monet to come to his château and paint the portrait of his wife, and Monet had to leave Camille something so that she could stay on at the hotel. But at last, for the first time for years, the letters to Bazille reveal a mind at rest, a happy person. 'Thanks to this gentleman from Le Havre who came to my help,' he wrote in the autumn, 'I have now no worries whatever. This is what I should like, always to stay like this, in a quiet little corner of the country-side. I am surrounded by all the things I love. I pass my time out of doors or on the shingle when the weather is stormy and there are big waves, also when the fishing boats go out. In the evening, my dear friend, I find a good fire and my dear little family waiting for me in my little house. Your godson is so well behaved just now. It is enchanting to watch the little creature grow, and I am so glad he is mine. I am going to paint him for the Salon with some other people round him, as is only right and proper.' The picture alluded to here is the *Picnic* now in Frankfurt, which I have discussed in the first chapter of this book.

I was able, a few years ago, to get the Louvre to buy the *Portrait of Madame Gaudibert*, a picture which had remained in the family of the Havre shipowner since it was painted. What moving memories surround this work and how grateful we should be to that shipowner, sufficiently intelli-gent to realise Monet's qualities, and a patron wealthy enough to procure him a few months of happiness. One small detail reflects those quiet hours with his family. On the back of the canvas, traced in pencil, is a sketch for a project which got no further: an interior; two women with a child.

Monet's situation was, however, still not sufficiently bright to enable him to dispense with sacrificing earlier canvases. In the same letter to Bazille he still asks him to send more so that he may scrape off the paint: 'abandoned work, and a canvas from the year 60 on which I had painted some execrable flowers'. How many masterpieces of Monet have been lost to us through his poverty!

His respite from poverty was short. The next year, in August 1869, Monet was living in the suburbs of Paris at St-Michel, near Bougival. There were fresh letters to Bazille and new demands for money. 'Dear friend, would you like to know how we lived during the eight days I have been waiting for your letter? Well, ask Renoir, who brought us some of his own bread so that we should not die. For eight days, no bread, no wine, no kitchen fire, no light. It's appalling!' Monet's distress at this time is confirmed by Renoir who also wrote to Bazille in his usual rather light-hearted manner. 'I am at Monet's nearly every day, rather an ageing experience, between you and me, as on some days they don't eat.' Renoir himself was not much better off. 'I am doing practically nothing,' he said in the same letter, 'because I haven't got many colours. Perhaps things will improve this month. If they do I'll write to you.' He could not even afford a stamp for his letter. 'I can't stamp it. I only have a few sous in my pocket, which I want for my fare to Paris when I need it.' Renoir did not worry unduly, because he was with his parents. With his naturally sanguine temperament he always accepted his poverty with a smile. While Monet ground his teeth, raged, grumbled, threatened, Renoir made a joke of it. The same letters to Bazille reveal a characteristic of Renoir's which well accorded with his temperament. He was greedy. He also assailed Bazille, but it was to ask him to send some boxes of grapes which Lise found delicious and some wine, and to tell him not to forget to send some woodcock on his way back in October. Before ending another letter he wrote, 'I'll write more another time, but I'm hungry, and in front of me is some brill in white sauce.'

The friendship between Bazille and Monet was to keep this note of pathos to the end. Exasperated by the imperious way in which Monet kept asking for help, Bazille advised Monet to go to Le Havre on foot and take up some remunerative occupation like chopping wood. Profoundly hurt, Monet answered on September 25, 'This to say that I have not followed your advice ... to go on foot to Le Havre. I have been a trifle happier this month, compared to last, though I am still in a desperate state. I have sold a still-life and done some work. But now, as usual, I am stopped for lack of paints. You, lucky chap, will bring back plenty of pictures! I alone will have done nothing this year. It makes me furious against everyone, envious, wicked, raging. You tell me quite seriously that in my place you would chop wood. It's only people in your position who think along those lines, and if you were in mine, you would probably be more distressed than I am. It's harder than you think, and I bet you wouldn't chop wood. Here comes the winter, and the house is not pleasant for unfortunates like ourselves. Then comes the Salon. Alas, I shall not be there, because I have done nothing. I have indeed a dream, a picture of the baths of La Grenouillère, for which I have done some rough sketches which are no good, but it is a dream.' A few rough sketches which are no good ... We too think we are dreaming, for Monet's La Grenouillère sketches are among the finest of his pictures. But when we read in countless letters Monet's complaints in despairing tones of doing nothing worth while, we must remember that for him, as for Corot, these sketches are not the aim and object of painting. What counted was the composition, which showed the Salon the painter's qualities. Rebuffed, however, by the Salon, ground down by poverty, Monet, after the disaster to the *Picnic* and *Women in the Garden* no longer dared undertake large-scale canvases.

Monet, who on June 26, 1870, married Camille, had someone to look after, Pissarro even more so, for by that time he already had two children. He was living at Louveciennes. How? We hardly know. He probably had difficulties like those of Monet. He had not, as Monet had, the resource of being able to tap Bazille over and over again. It is curious to observe how these artists continued to group themselves according to the pattern of their early meetings. Renoir, Monet, Sisley, and Bazille kept till 1870 the camaraderie they had developed in Gleyre's studio, Pissarro reserved his affection for another group, that of the Académie Suisse, which included Cézanne and Guillaumin.

Art lovers and patrons were then rare birds, and dealers very few. Manet had already done business with Martinet. The Impressionists sold their work through Latouche. He had a small shop at the corner of the Rue Lafitte. They also dealt more especially with 'Father' Martin, Corot's agent, also Boudin's and Jongkind's. Martin paid the highest prices (100 francs) for

CAMILLE PISSARRO *Self-portrait*

Monet's work, and for Pissarro's 30 to 40 francs according to size.

The Franco-Prussian war of 1870 and the Commune scattered all these artists who previously had met each other regularly at the Café Guerbois, not far from Manet's studio in the Batignolles. Manet and Degas joined the National Guard. Cézanne fled to L'Estaque near Marseilles. At the end of 1870 Monet and Pissarro were in London where Daubigny introduced them to his agent Durand-Ruel.

Pissarro had to flee in haste from his studio at Louveciennes, leaving behind the greater part of the work he had done since 1855 and several pictures which Monet had asked him to keep. This precious hoard met with disaster. The Prussians installed a butchery in the house. They did not use the canvases as aprons, as has been said, but as carpets in the garden to keep their feet clean. This hecatomb, which affected Pissarro and added to all the misfortunes already undergone by Monet, helps to explain the rarity

PAUL CÉZANNE *Self-portrait*   ARMAND GUILLAUMIN *Self-portrait*

of works by the Impressionists before 1870.

After the war, the position seemed a little better. The new school of painting had its agent, Durand-Ruel, who had hitherto sold Corot and the Romantics but now became interested in Manet. In London, in 1871, he had already bought two of Pissarro's pictures for 200 francs each, and went up to 300 for pictures by Monet. Back in Paris in 1872, he bought, in two transactions, thirty-two pictures by Manet, whom he paid from 400 to 3,000 francs, 15,000 francs altogether, bargain prices it must be confessed. The next year Manet sold five pictures, including the *Bon Bock,* which had just had a success at the Salon, for prices varying from 2,500 francs to 6,000 francs. Art lovers began to take an interest in the Impressionists. Théodore Duret preferred Manet. Degas sold to Rouart, a businessman and also a childhood friend, and to Valpinçon. Caillebotte, Hoschedé, Dr. Gachet, were discriminating purchasers, as were the brothers Hecht. In 1894,

EDOUARD MANET *Portrait of Théodore Duret*

Hoschedé, a director of a big shop in Paris, was obliged to hold an auction at the Hôtel Drouot. There a Degas fetched 1,100 francs, the Sisleys and Monets averaged 400 to 500 francs, a landscape of Pissarro's reached 950 francs.

The nucleus of patrons, which gradually spread, and the support of a first-class dealer, helped Impressionism slowly to gain a foothold; only a little patience was needed. Unfortunately that was just the virtue these artists so conspicuously lacked, though one must admit that they had all passed their youth, and that their urge to see their talents recognised by their countrymen was therefore perfectly legitimate.

In 1874, Boudin was 50, Pissarro 44, Manet 42, Degas 40, Cézanne 35, Monet 34. The possibility of their being shown at the Salon depended on the caprice of a Hanging Committee, which, after the war, tended to become more and more severe. They therefore had long discussions among themselves as to the chances of forming a group to show their work, a proposal

GUSTAVE CAILLEBOTTE *Self-portrait*

which had already been ventilated before the war, in a suggestion of Bazil-le's made in 1867.

In 1874, the proposal was taken up again by Monet who was always a fighter. Durand-Ruel was in difficulties at the beginning of 1874, and had to cancel his purchases, and the artists were looking for a way out. Pissarro took up Monet's idea enthusiastically. His socialist opinions inclined him to a syndicalist turn of mind and nothing could please him more than the idea of a group of modern painters in close association. Théodore Duret, who was a good prophet, tried to wean him from this project, saying that the only way to achieve fame was via the Salon and the sales at the Hôtel Drouot. Degas wanted to soften the aggressive character of the venture by mixing nuclei of moderns among more conformist painters. Berthe Morisot, who had never been refused by the Salon, agreed as a good friend. As to Manet, he categorically condemned the enterprise. His success at the 1873 Salon, with the *Bon Bock,* was not calculated to make him forgo the chance of official honours. Although a convinced republican, he never was, where art was concerned, made of revolutionary stuff, and for him the Salon was the only true battlefield for the artist. The presence of Cézanne among the rebels confirmed him in his distaste. He told Monet, 'I would never compromise myself with that fellow!' Fantin-Latour followed Manet. Corot, who only had a few months to live, looked askance at this rebellion against the Salon. To Guillemet, who had been asked to take part in the demonstration, Corot is reputed to have said, 'My dear Antoine, you're well out of it, believe me, with that crowd!' One hundred and sixty pictures were shown at the 'Exhibition of the Co-operative Society of Artist-Painters, Sculptors, Engravers, etc.' which was open from April 15 till May 15, 1874, in the rooms of the aeronaut-photographer, Nadar, at 31 Boulevard des Capucines. The alphabetical list shows a curious mixture: Astruc, Attendu, Beliard, Boudin, Bracquemond, Brandon, Bureau, Cals, Cézanne, Colin, Debras, Degas, Latouche, Lepic, Levert, Meyer, de Molins, Monet, Berthe Morisot, Mulot-Durivage, A. Ottin, P. L. Ottin, Pissarro, Renoir, Robert, Rouart, Sisley! Grouped thus, and despite the presence of the 'hostages'

HENRI FANTIN-LATOUR *Homage to Delacroix*

CLAUDE MONET *Impression: sunrise*

insisted on by Degas, the Impressionists certainly shocked the public quite as much as Monet and Pissarro hoped, but the shock took the form of a colossal scandal which alienated art lovers instead of converting them.

The only thing the group gained was its name, given it by the critic Larcy, after Monet's picture *Impression of Sunrise*. Subsequent exhibitions, especially that of 1876, repelled people even more.

Monet and Pissarro's plan was a mistake. It was not a good idea just after the war of 1870 to show oneself a revolutionary. Memories of the Commune were still only too vivid, and Paris was with difficulty rising from the ruins it had made. The middle classes, therefore, came down on everything which dared to 'rise up' against accepted ideas. The result, for the Impressionist painters, was a new economic crisis, to which was added the horrid feeling of being treated as pariahs. However, some patrons stuck to them and they even acquired new ones, such as Dr. de Bellio, Georges Charpentier, the publisher, Count Armand Doria, Ernest May. These were highly enthusiastic. Count Armand Doria was at Nadar's looking at the exhibits with his son François. Seeing Cézanne's contribution, he said to his son, 'There is first-class work here. I must have something by this painter.' He bought the *House of the Hanged Man* (page 197). It was Cézanne who, in 1876, caused the loudest laughter among the visitors, but who, nevertheless, collected another fanatical admirer in Monsieur Choquet. He held the humble position of principal clerk at the customs head office. He was the original of Zola's Monsieur Hue in *L'Œuvre*. He had succeeded, at a small outlay, in collecting a magnificent group of pictures by Delacroix, his favourite artist. But at the Impressionists' sale in 1875 he was thunderstruck at his first view of modern painting. He commissioned Renoir to paint his wife, and through him got to know Cézanne, who speedily became his favourite. At the Impressionists' exhibitions he constituted himself a guide, trying to persuade the visitors to buy his friend's pictures. He bought not less than thirty-two Cézannes. Nor did he rest till he had got the *House of the Hanged Man* away from Count Doria. He exchanged it for another picture by Cézanne. He did not, however, pay much for his pictures. Round about 1885/86 he inherited some money, bought a mansion and stopped collecting. He confessed to Renoir: 'Now I am no longer interested in buying pictures, because I know I have only to take out my wallet.' A real art lover!

The exhibition having had the sole result, on the financial side, of forcing the Society to go into liquidation, the artists found themselves obliged to have a sale at the Hôtel Drouot to make some money. Coming so soon after the scandal of the preceding year, this could only end in disaster. The sale realised 11,491 francs, including work bought back by the artists themselves. They had obtained less than half the price their pictures had previously fetched and the annoyance of the public had so much increased that the auctioneer had to call in the police. At the sale of the Hoschedé collection, which took place after this, the prices were the lowest the Impressionists had ever known. Manets went for 500 to 800 francs, Monets from 50 to 505 francs, three Renoirs fetched 51 francs, 42, and 84. A Pissarro went for 7 and another for 10 francs. Pissarro, discouraged, declared, 'the Hoschedé sale has finished me off!'

The years 1874 to 1880 were, therefore, particularly hard for these artists. They went round ringing front door bells and offering their wares at rock-bottom prices in the hope of inducing some more people to support them. Sisley, as a result of his father having ruined himself, joined the poverty-stricken band. Pissarro, penniless, took refuge in 1874 at the house of his friend Ludovic Piette at Montfoucault, and took his family with him. Monet became famous for being 'always on the look out for a gold *louis*'.

In the thesis, unfortunately not published, written in 1955 for the Ecole du Louvre by Monsieur Michel Rostand on 'Some art lovers of the Impressionist period', we find piteous letters from Monet, dated 1878 or 1879, and others from Pissarro and Sisley, to almost all the collectors of Impressionist pictures. One of these is particularly moving, because it shows how great the mental distress of these artists was and how low their morale could fall. In September 1879 Camille died. On the 5th Monet wrote to Dr. de Bellio to ask for some money with which to redeem from the pawn shop her medallion. 'It was the only souvenir my wife was able to keep and I should like to put it round her neck before we part.' On February 18 Monet had sold to de Bellio the fine *Gare St-Lazare* (page 155), which de Bellio's daughter subsequently gave to the Musée Marmottan, for 65 francs!

The artists were, then, reduced to offering their work at absurdly low prices. Between 1877 and 1880 Monet suggested that Chocquet should buy from him 'one or two odds and ends' for 50 or 40 francs. Pissarro offered his for 50, or even 20 francs. 'For a week I've been running round Paris trying to find the type of man who will buy Impressionist pictures', he wrote in June 1878. Some strange combinations came into force; for instance, in 1878, Manet told Théodore Duret that Monet's situation was so critical that he had asked him (Manet) to find someone who would take ten or twenty pictures for 100 francs each. Manet went on, 'Would you like us to go in together and give, say, 500 francs each?' But Duret did not respond to this suggestion and Manet 'went it alone', giving Monet a signed receipt for 1,000 francs, 'the value of the merchandise'. Such expedients as lotteries were even tried. The big prize was a picture by Pissarro, and the affair was organised from the shop of Murer, the pastrycook-restaurateur. The little maid who won the picture exchanged it for a medal of St-Honoré.

Their financial embarrassments were increased by inevitable additions to their families. At the beginning of February 1878 Camille was about to have a second child. Monet seems to have made the tour of his friends. There are two letters to Dr. Gachet, one of February 9, appealing for help, the other of the 15th asking once more for 100 francs and offering to 'repay with a picture'. When Camille was brought to bed he wrote, in March, to Ernest May asking an advance of 300, 200, or even 100 francs. In November of the same year, it was Pissarro whose wife was in labour and who was appealing to Murer. He must leave Pontoise and only has 200 francs, from a picture he has sold, for the move. The old fighter was losing heart. In an earlier letter to Murer he wrote: 'Want, even destitution, prevails with us, and menaces my family all the time. It's no longer bearable. When shall I get out of this mess! I feel as if I were stifling in a flour bin! I work without rhyme or reason, without joy, without enthusiasm, because of this feeling that I ought to give up art and look for something else, if it is possible to learn a new trade at my age! How sad it all is!'

Sometimes it happened that in their begging they were competing with one another. One day Monet arrived at the house of a possible patron, only to be told by the butler: 'You haven't a hope. Monsieur Sisley has just called.'

In 1880 the position was no better. Monet, now living at Vétheuil, asked Duret for 100 francs on March 8. On August 6 he received a summons from 'an old creditor'. He 'hadn't a *sou to* give him' and to escape seizure of his goods he asked Charpentier the publisher to pay now a sum he was to have paid him the following April.

Renoir, at least, was a little better off. He had had a great success at the Salon with the *Portrait of Madame Charpentier and her Children* (Metropolitan Museum, New York) which the judges had let in out of regard for the famous publisher. He got 1,000 francs for it in 1879, which, after all, was not very much considering the size of the canvas. Thanks, however, to his visits to Madame Charpentier's salon, he had made a reputation as a society painter. They sent him young children to paint, and he thereby acquired some means, and no longer had to write to de Bellio or Théodore Duret to send him 100 francs to pay his rent.

These long sad years provoked quarrels among art lovers, critics, dealers and artists, and between the artists themselves quarrels amounting to brawls. These could go very far. In 1869, as a result of a quarrel at the Café Guerbois, Duranty and Manet fought a duel. Degas and Manet, both very irritable people, gave each other back pictures they had originally given to each other, and Degas fell into a rage when he saw that Manet had cut out that part of the canvas on which he had painted Manet's wife playing the piano beside her husband. On another occasion it was Monet and Manet who got angry with one another. (They admired each other but never had much in common.) Manet returned to Monet the *Women in the Garden,* which he had exchanged with Bazille's father for a portrait of the latter by Renoir.

By about 1890, after thirty years of struggle, the first generation of Impressionists had won through at last. An old age preserved from the sordid

PAUL CÉZANNE *Portrait of Victor Chocquet*

anxieties of daily life was at least granted to those who had passed the best years of their lives in poverty. The vision of the world which they had insisted on had become so commonplace that the officials who had chased them from the portals of the Salon were now making a good thing out of them. Everyone had discovered their technique. All of which made Degas, always sarcastic, say: 'They shoot us, and they rob us too.'

The army of martyrs was not, however, without new recruits. Other fighters stepped into the breach and carried the fight further forward than their elders had done, going beyond, even, those appearances which the latter had not only respected but rejoiced at. There were three of them, Seurat, Gauguin, and Van Gogh. All three died young and in tragic circumstances, while the old Impressionists, Cézanne, Degas, Renoir, Pissarro, Monet, lived to great ages, playing the parts of the patriarchs of the art-world after having been the young rebels. Is it to be concluded that to be on intimate

PAUL GAUGUIN *Self-portrait à l'idole* (detail)

terms with nature has a soothing influence, while the passion to penetrate the mystery lying behind appearances provokes expenditure of nervous energy, which ultimately wears out the body and soul? Seurat died at thirty-one of an infectious angina contracted when preparing for the Salon des Indépendents of 1890. We may think that the harassing labour involved in Seurat's method reduced his body to a poor state of defence and hastened his end. How did he live? Doubtless on allowances from his family, as he only sold two pictures. His instincts were middle-class, but he led a veritable hermit's life, in conformity with the purism of his painting. His studio had white walls, was completely devoid of furniture, and adorned only with pictures.

Respectable people, the artists of whom we have spoken up to now were good husbands and good fathers. Their life conformed to bourgeois morals in all respects. Their poverty irked them especially, because it prevented them

VINCENT VAN GOGH *Self-portrait dedicated to Gauguin*

living that normal life, that stable existence, to which, like all the men of their age, they aspired. It was quite different with Gauguin and Van Gogh. It was these two madmen who started the rupture between the artist and society. To the twentieth century they were the models for geniuses beyond the law, possessed by superhuman powers, which at the same time laid them low.

Like an unattainable paradise, Van Gogh longed for that domesticity which he called 'the true life' and which he banished from his dreams in order to paint. Gauguin, who had known it, sacrificed it to his genius, though he missed it sometimes. His letters to his wife reveal his unfailing attachment to his family: after years of affliction, he liked to project a mirage of repose among those he loved on the horizon of his unhappy life. However, the ordeal could not be avoided. Bohemianism had been the way of life of nineteenth-century artists, but with Van Gogh and Gauguin came another style, that of the *saison en enfer* already tried out by Rimbaud.

51

AUGUSTE RENOIR *Portrait of Vollard*   VINCENT VAN GOGH *Portrait of Père Tan,*

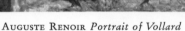

Whoever wants to create must first break every link with his surroundings, accept that he is damned, penetrate blindfold into the raging Gehenna where he will hear his voices. Utrillo, Modigliani and Soutine were to follow this course in the next century.

If Gauguin had been Monet, he would not have known this hell. As a former stock-broker, his private means, though limited, should have helped him await the arrival of success. During the Tahiti period the dealers were dancing attendance: Portier, Tanguy, Goupil and then Vollard; and soon the collectors Fayet, Charles Morice and Monfreid were all regularly buying up his works. Discovered by a miracle, the accounts·he kept at Atuana show that Gauguin was spending about nine hundred pounds a year there in to-day's currency. Thus Gauguin willingly plunged into the abyss, gripped by an urge to reject with hate and violence all that was middle-class, while freeing the power of his genius by a shock-treatment which caused it to well up from springs long buried under the sands of civilization.

Several times during the course of history the balance of a mind too delicately poised has not resisted the terrible impact of genius: Francesco Bas-

AUGUSTE RENOIR *Portrait of Charles and Georges Durand-Ruel*

sano, Borromini and nearer our times Jongkind, not to mention the classic example of Nietzsche, all sank into madness. To this form of martyrdom Van Gogh was assigned. Not that his was the painting of a madman; for apart from one or two doubtful cases his works are always magnificently conceived, and do not reveal that discordance of elements found in the painting of the insane. He, on the contrary, fought against madness to free his genius.

It would be tedious to continue the recitation of this martyrology. The few examples I have given are enough to show the courage needed by these artists to fight poverty for so many years, and also stupidity and indifference. After 1881, dire poverty became indigence. Manet's posthumous sales in February 1884 ensured his success after his death. There were still ups and downs, depending on uncertain economic factors and the vicissitudes of Durand-Ruel's business. But at last they could see daylight at the end of the tunnel. How touching is Renoir's naiveté when in 1887, at the age of forty-six, he was astonished, just like a child, at success. 'The public seems to be coming in,' he wrote to Durand-Ruel on May 13. 'Maybe I'm wrong, but

EDOUARD MANET *Lunch in the studio*

everyone says so. Why now and not before? There seems to be no reason.'

The new fervour for Impressionism is naturally reflected in the prices. It is enough to compare the prices reached by the same picture at twenty year intervals to realise this. *Déjeuner dans l'Atelier*, bought by Faure for 4,000 francs from Manet in 1874, was sold by him for 22,500 francs to Durand-Ruel in 1894. It was Durand-Ruel again who, in 1898, bought Manet's *Picnic* for 20,000 francs from Faure. Faure had paid 3,000 francs for it in 1878. At the end of the nineteenth and start of the twentieth century, de Camondo was getting together the collection he eventually left to the Louvre, and paid good prices: 20,000 francs for Monet's *London, Houses of Parliament* in 1906, and in 1907 25,000 francs for the *Blue Vase* by Cézanne which he paid to Jacques Pot, 30,000 francs for one of the same artist's still-lifes to Bernheim-Jeune, and finally 43,000 francs for Sisley's *Flood at Port Marly* (page 171) at the Tavernier sale in 1900. Sisley, alas, never knew even the moral satisfaction of success. We know little about him, for he lived retired, obscure, a prey to melancholy, resigned never to know fame, having all the same the feeling that it would come to him after his death. He was right. A year after he had gone (January 29, 1899) the prices of his pictures began to rise.

From 1900 onwards, the price of Impressionist pictures bought in Germany, Switzerland, and the U.S.A., continued to rise. Already in 1907 the Metropolitan Museum in New York had paid 92,000 francs for the *Portrait of Madame Charpentier and her Children* by Renoir. At the Rouart sale in 1912, a picture by Degas, *Dancers at the Practice Bar,* realised the highest amount paid for an Impressionist work before the 1914 war, the huge sum of 435,000 francs. It is claimed that this was the result of a mistake; an American collector is said to have selected two agents who outbid each other at the expense of the purchaser! For the artists who, for thirty years, had been obliged to live in obscurity, and in the case of some of them in misery, this astronomical rise in the prices of pictures which they had formerly sold for some hundreds of francs, seemed bitter.

Zola, who later went back on his early enthusiasm for the Impressionists, was a good prophet when in his article in the *Evénément* in 1866, he wrote, apropos of Manet, 'I would consider I had done a good stroke of business, if I had the money, in buying to-day all his pictures. In ten years they will be selling for fifteen and twenty times as much.'

ON THE THRESHOLD OF IMMORTALITY

RIDICULED by the critics, spat on by the public, rejected by the judges at the various Salons, the Impressionists, whose pictures were not bought for the Nation like those of other artists still living, risked not having later on the place at the Louvre to which they were entitled. For that place to be won, several fine Frenchmen had to expend their energy and generosity, often meeting with resistance from officialdom.

In order to understand these matters one must know how the enrichment of public collections by the work of living artists is managed in France. It is to the administration of the Fine Arts at the time of Louis XVIII that we owe the foundation of a museum specially devoted to contemporary art. To contribute to the ornamentation of the House of Lords and bring to life the Left Bank, the Royal Museum of the Luxembourg for the Work of Living Artists was installed in the palace of that name. It was solemnly opened on April 24, 1818. The chief decoration was the collection of large compositions by David, two of which, the *Leonidas* and the *Sabine Women,* were bought from the regicide painter by the royal administration. From 1818 till our own time the policy governing acquisitions has been essentially based on eclecticism. But when it wants to appear liberal, the administration stops selecting, and welcomes all tendencies. This is why when it makes good buys they are always fewer than the bad ones. More often, however, it asks for guidance from the judges at the Salon, where anyhow most of the purchases are made, and it will practise the same policy of ostracising original talent. Prud'hon's work was shown at the Luxembourg from the start, Delacroix came in 1822 with the *Barque de Dante,* Ingres in 1823. During the reign of Louis-Philippe, the judges at the Salon were particularly severe, only welcoming pictures inspired by the official aesthetic of the moment. The administration did as it was told, and it was only in 1852 that Théodore Rousseau reached the Luxembourg, and Corot in 1855. Chassériau arrived only in 1863, and Courbet after 1871.

At the moment when the question of admitting the Impressionists, whose pictures private persons were seeking to donate, came up, the Museum of Living Artists changed its abode. The Senate, sitting hitherto at Versailles, took possession of the Luxembourg in 1879 and evicted the museum, which was transferred to the former Orangery in the garden, which, as it had overhead lighting, fulfilled the requirements of the day for a modern museum. It was opened in 1886, offering a mural surface of 2,406 yards for the pictures, and a space of 473 yards for the sculpture.

The Nation had bought so many pictures by the end of the nineteenth century, there being so many artists, that the Curators Committee decided that, so far as the Luxembourg was concerned, not more than three pictures by the same painter would be accepted. Later when foreign artists were admitted, the pictures were taken to the former Jeu de Paume of the Tuileries, overlooking the Place de la Concorde. This transfer was decided upon by Monsieur Paul Léon, the Director of Fine Arts, and it took place in the spring of 1922.

For its funds the Luxembourg Museum was in an ambiguous position. It received a subvention from the Civil List under the monarchical regime, also funds from the Fine Arts administration, and a lesser sum from the Museums administration. Under the Third Republic it was above all the duty of the Fine Arts administration to provide for the growth of the Luxembourg Museum. At the beginning of the twentieth century, the Museums Council strictly forbade the buying of the work of living artists. The sometimes more enlightened taste of the curators of the National Museums was powerless before the hostile attitude of both the Museums Council and the Fine Arts administration.

As to the distribution of the work of living artists, there was no written rule. For the best, considered worthy of the Louvre, there was an unwritten rule that it could not pass through the portals of that august institution until they had been dead ten years. This rule had, however, been broken in the case of specially famous artists. Thus the pictures of Ingres and Delacroix did not wait ten years from the death of their creators, to pass on from the Luxembourg to the Louvre. For donations and legacies, their acceptance by the Nation, permitted by decree, was, before 1896, submitted to the Museums Consultative Committee, a body composed of curators of the National Museums which, before 1914, were few in number. When the 'Reunion of National Museums' came into being in 1895, a body with both civil and moral influence, it was looked after financially by an administrative council called the 'Museums Council' which started functioning in 1896 under the chairmanship of Count de Laborde. On April 5,

EDGAR DEGAS *Portrait of Léon Bonnat*

1897, the minister decided that the donations and legacies in kind should be submitted for approval to the Museums Council also. Since 1945, some of the powers of the Museums Council have been divided between two bodies, the Administrative Council and the Artistic Council. Since 1897, at least, all acquisitions by the museums, whether paid for or given, must be submitted for approval to two more bodies, the Committee of Curators and the Museums Council. This does not, however, include acquisitions paid for out of current account, which are left by the Council to the sole disposal of the curators. But these small purchases were, during the first years, closely scrutinised by the members of the Council. Before the last reform the Council was supreme. Since the Decree of July 13, 1955, the minister can override the Council's decision.

During the period which is of interest for us, the Chairman of the Museums Council was Léon Bonnat. Originally Vice-Chairman, he was elected Chairman at the meeting of May 8, 1899, after the resignation of the Count de Laborde. He continued as Chairman until his death in 1922. It is therefore impossible to deny that his baneful influence lasted over a long period.

Born in Bayonne, Léon Bonnat made his first appearance as a painter of historical scenes in 1860. His passion was strongly inspired by the Spanish masters (like Manet), but he preferred Ribera to Velasquez. After the Franco-Prussian war of 1870, he took up portraiture, for which there was an enormous demand among the middle classes. In dreary colours, dominated by dark brown, Léon Bonnat painted all the leading personalities of State and of the bourgeoisie. He devoted the fortune thus amassed to collecting pictures, especially old drawings, which he bequeathed to Bayonne and to the Louvre. He had the reputation of being a perspicacious art lover. But keeping to the official code of aesthetics in vogue at the Ecole des Beaux-Arts, of which he was director, he regarded modern art with a contempt which never relaxed.

The first passage at arms with the Government over the entrance of Impressionist pictures into the public collections began with the gift of Manet's *Olympia*. We know a great deal of what went on, because Gustave Geffroy, in his monograph on Monet, has published the correspondence. The suggestion that this picture should be bought by public subscription and given to the Nation came from Monet, always a fighter, who all his life had a firm dislike of officials. He refused the Legion of Honour, and in 1890 he wrote to Geffroy apropos the article by Antonin Proust in the *Figaro*, which we shall discuss latter, 'I wrote to Proust and told him what I thought of him. There is no coming to terms with people like that. I want nothing to do with them or their Crosses.' Antonin Proust was a friend of Manet, and, when a minister, had got him a decoration. Now his attitude was somewhat ambiguous. He sent 500 francs to Monet as a subscription, while at the same time appearing to blame him for undertaking the venture. As often happens in such cases, the disagreement was increased by the journalists, the *Figaro* having published an interview with Proust, in which the latter was made to say that his subscription had been meant to help Manet's widow, whose situation was described as 'the saddest and most lamentable that can be imagined'. Proust, however, himself wrote in the *République* in terms unfavourable to the project, which caused Monet to say: 'He must find it worth while to wait till the Manets sell for 500,000 francs, to buy them.' The thing went so far that, according to the code

EDOUARD VUILLARD *Toulouse Lautrec at Villeneuve-sur-Yonne*

of honour of the time, Proust challenged Monet to a duel. Théodore Duret and Gustave Geffroy, Monet's seconds, were happily able to arrange a moving reconciliation between the two old friends.

Monet sent to Fallières, the Minister of Public Instruction, and later President of France, the list of subscribers with a letter making a gift of the *Olympia* to the Louvre, on condition it was not left waiting at the Luxembourg until the period of ten years from the death of the artist had expired. After lengthy correspondence with the administration, Monet ended it by giving his consent to an acceptance of the donation with no strings attached as to the future of the picture once it had reached the Luxembourg.

It is interesting to look at the list of subscribers. The amount subscribed reached 19,114 francs out of the 20,000 needed. All Manet's artist friends of the early years were of course included, except Sisley, whose absence was perhaps accounted for by his poverty. Fantin-Latour, Degas, Guillemet, Bracquemond, Caillebotte, Toulouse-Lautrec, Pissarro, Monet, Raffaelli, Rodin, Renoir. As well as these, however, there were artists who had made a name for themselves at the Salon, and who admired Impressionism without having adopted its methods, such as Duez, Léon Lhermitte, Jules Chéret, Jean Béraud, Ribot, Puvis de Chavannes, Carolus-Duran, Dalou, Boldini, Gervex, Carrière, Friant, Helleu, Roll, Tissot, Rops, J. E. Blanche. There were few dealers' names: Durand-Ruel, Georges Petit, Portier; a good many art lovers: the bankers Hecht, Georges Murer, de Bellio, Paul Gallimard, Moreau-Nélaton, Rouart, Eugène Blot, Lerolle, Théodore Duret; among critics: Roger Marx, Armand Dayot, Philippe Burty; writers: Marcel Bernstein, Octave Mirbeau, Mallarmé, Gustave Geffroy, Huysmans. There were also two composers, Clapisson and Emmanuel Chabrier, who collected Impressionist pictures. These were the politicians who subscribed: Alexandre Millerand, Antonin Proust, Camille Pelletan. Léon Bourgeois, Minister of Public Instruction, received the donation in the name of the Nation. Later on he was a member of the Museums Council. Gustave Geffroy published several of the letters sent by subscribers. These are warmhearted and moving when they come from sincere friends like Rodin, Renoir, Duez, obliged to send only a small sum because of their poverty. There are also letters of refusal. That of Joseph Reinach explains itself, but what of Zola's, full of wounding remarks? He had been the one to foresee the splendid rise in value of the Impressionist pictures, and he

AUGUSTE RENOIR *Two girls at the piano*

now accused Monet of having had commercial ends in view, in a process of reasoning often used later by detractors of modern art: 'Let the art lovers get together, if they want to,' he said, 'to send up the prices of a painter whose pictures they all possess. I understand their motive, but I, as a writer, will have nothing to do with it.'

A proof that the price of 20,000 francs asked for the *Olympia* in 1890 was not exorbitant, is that at the Meissonier sale in 1893, one of this painter's canvases went for 272,000 francs. Monet knew about prices, for in 1889, at the Secretan sale, Meissonier being still alive, one of his pictures fetched 190,000 francs, and another had fetched 336,000 francs in New York in 1887. Zola in the generous period of his youth had fought for Impressionism, because, as a modern writer, he upheld modern art, in which he saw naturalistic tendencies similar to his own. But, as his book *L'Œuvre* shows, he was a literary man above all and understood little about art.

Olympia was hung in the Orangery of the Luxembourg. The administration began to be aware of the existence of Impressionism. In 1892 it bought Renoir's *Girls at the Piano,* and Fantin-Latour's great iconographic picture, the *Studio at the Batignolles,* which was, as it were, the first manifesto of the group. *Girl at the Ball* by Berthe Morisot was acquired at the suggestion of Mallarmé at the Théodore Duret sale of March 19, 1894. Impressionism was recognised by the administration as having a place in the Museum of Living Artists, but a very small place compared with the enormous spaces occupied by the official artists. Thirty years later, all these latter pictures vanished into the attics of the museums of France. However, when the Caillebotte legacy confronted the authorities with the entry of sixty-seven pictures by Impressionist artists, the whole question came up again, hostilities were resumed against Impressionism, and there was a crisis.

In her thesis on 'Gustave Caillebotte. His Work and his Collection' which was accepted by the Ecole du Louvre, Mademoiselle Marie Bérhaud, to-day Curator of the Rennes Museum, collected and analysed all she could find in the archives on the affair of the Caillebotte legacy, which nevertheless still remains an obscure enough business. Gustave Caillebotte, who, as a painter, had always faithfully taken part in the Impressionist exhibitions, began the collection of pictures which his fortune enabled him to make, shortly after 1870. He continued to collect till 1888. It has too often been repeated that his buys were dictated by generosity and that the Impressionists gave him those canvases which they found hardest to sell. In reality they were all 'unsaleable' during the heroic epoch. Caillebotte simply had an *embarras de choix,* but this choice was singularly correct when he kept such works as Manet's *Balcony* (see page 122), the *Moulin de la Galette* (see page 178), *Nude in the Sunlight* (see page 181), *Woman Reading* (see page 184), or *Swing* (see page 180) of Renoir, the *Gare St-Lazare* (see page 155), or *Regatta at Argenteuil* (see page 153) of Monet, *The Red Roofs* (see page 164), or the *Côte d'Hermitage* of Pissarro, and *L'Estaque* by Cézanne (see page 202).

The Caillebotte legacy, comprising the whole collection, was the object of two wills. In the first, dated 1876, in view of the fact that the Nation would not be able immediately to take possession, and not for a period which he estimated at some twenty years, the testator laid down that the pictures should be looked after by his brother, Martial, but that they should be exhibited in 1878 at the expense of the heirs. A second will of November 28, 1883, took no account of this transitory period, but kept the clause that the pictures should not vegetate 'in some attic or in a provincial museum'.

Acquisitions by the museums were at that time submitted for approval to a single body, the Consultative Committee, consisting of the curators, of whom there were not yet very many. The minutes of the committee meeting of March 22, to which the terms of the legacy were submitted, do not permit us, by their briefness, to know what arguments took place. But on the proposal of Léonce Bénédite, Curator of the Luxembourg Museum, the committee pronounced in favour of accepting the whole of the legacy and placing it in the Luxembourg together with a picture by Caillebotte himself, the *Floor Polishers*, which the heirs had added to the rest. The minister authorised on April 27 the acceptance of this picture, but said not a word about the legacy. As Marie Bérhaud has shown, the difficulties seem to have arisen not from the administration of the Fine Arts but from political circles, and they were, as so frequently happens, exacerbated by the press, who hurled themselves into an affair which would have done better for being discussed in the privacy of the minister's room. In April, however, the *Journal des Arts* started an enquiry to get the opinions of 'the artists most loved by the public'. One can guess what these were! The administration, therefore, now became aware that the Luxembourg was too small to receive the whole collection, and that it was not to be used for living artists or for exhibition of so great a quantity of works by a single individual. We have seen above that the number of pictures by the same artist which could be accepted had been reduced to three. After complicated negotiations between Renoir, who was one of the executors, Martial Caillebotte, brother of the deceased, Henri de Roujon, a Director of Museums, Léonce Bénédite, Curator of the Luxembourg, and the lawyers, it was decided to compromise and accept thirty-eight out of sixty-seven pictures offered.

The way in which the choice was made leaves pretty clear the taste of the curators of the period. They did not want to be invaded by a large number of pictures by Monet, Sisley, and above all Pissarro. Pissarro was the chief victim with eleven pictures refused. His reputation was lower than Monet's who was considered to be more creative. As regards the Cézannes, it is understandable that they should not have wanted the *Women Bathing*. Cubism had to come before it could be appreciated. Cézanne was, in fact, the one who was for longest misunderstood. He suffered the largest amputation, three out of five. Of Manet's pictures, one wonders what could be amiss with that charming picture, *The Croquet Players*. Finally the fact that all the Degas were accepted shows that in official circles the taint of the revolutionary which rested on all the other Impressionists was not considered to have touched him. Léonce Bénédite valued the collection at 140,000 francs. In the light of the prices which Manet and Monet were getting even then, this was clearly underestimating these works. The valuation of 500,000 francs put on it by the Caillebotte family was much more exact.

Here is a comparative and quantitative table of the works bequeathed and accepted.

Name	Bequeathed	Accepted	Refused
Renoir	8	6	2
Cézanne	5	2	3
Degas	7	7	—
Manet	4	2	2
Monet	16	8	8
Pissarro	18	7	11
Sisley	9	6	3
Total	67	38	29

Placed in the foreground by events, the curators of museums are too often judged by the public as being responsible for situations over which in fact they have not sole control. An official, generally speaking, is only responsible to public opinion for his mistakes. The credit for his successes always goes to someone higher up the ladder. One recalls Marshal Joffre's remark, after the victory of the Marne in 1916: 'I don't know who has won this battle. But I know who would have been blamed if it had been lost.' It is only the more objective historian who can try to get at the facts. Therefore let us give Léonce Bénédite, Curator of the Luxembourg, his due. Still to-day he is being accused of having been responsible for the mutilation of the Caillebotte legacy. On the contrary, throughout the negotiations, he tried to get the collection accepted in its totality, suggesting, by way of compromise, that there should be a temporary exhibition of part of the pictures at Versailles and Compiègne. Unfortunately, these museums were considered by the Caillebotte family's legal adviser as 'provincial museums'. One should not forget either that Lefenestre, Curator of Paintings at the Louvre, and a member of the Institut de France, refused to sign the letter of protest put out by the Academy of Fine Arts, and protested at its being sent to the minister. As for Henri de Roujon, his position as liaison between the minister and the curators confined him to a cautious attitude, but he replied in moderate, but none the less energetic, terms to the questions asked in the Senate on the subject of the admission of the collection to the Luxembourg. To sum up, although the Caillebotte collection was in part refused, it was the fault not so much of the Fine Arts administration as of public opinion, as expressed in the press, and also of the Institut with its great authority.

This muttering of protest broke into a roar when the 'scandal' saw the light of day and the Caillebotte collection was put on view at the Luxembourg at the beginning of February, 1896. By 18 votes to 10, among which was, Lefenestre's, the Academy of Fine Arts decided to send the minister a protest. In it was the statement that the Luxembourg should be reserved 'for the best specimens of French art' (vanished to-day into oblivion) and that the presence of the Caillebotte collection was 'an offence to the dignity of our school'. At the very bottom of the document is the signature of one of the most erudite of Frenchmen, the Count de Laborde, Permanent Secretary of the Academy.

Invoking the high authority of the Academy of Fine Arts, Monsieur Hervé de Saisy, a Senator, questioned the Government on the admission of the 'unspeakable Caillebotte collection' into the 'sanctuary reserved for real artists, whose names posterity will acclaim'. The whole document is worth quoting, but we may mention at least that the *Olympia* was treated as vile and mean. As to the Argenteuil painters, they were chiefly reproached for painting landscapes in which the 'wind was the dominant factor'. This was apparently a mad thing to do, for 'the wind never wafted painters to the Capitol, but swept them to the edge of the Tarpeian Rock'. There must have been plenty of wind in this gentleman's head! It is a sobering thought that it was nonsense such as this with which these masterpieces were reviled! For some reason the minister did not reply himself but ordered Monsieur de Roujon to do so, as 'Government Commissioner', doubless in the name of the principles of the Civil Service, as I quoted above. In any case Roujon found apt words with which to end the argument. 'Though most of us consider that Impressionism is not the last word in art, we nevertheless agree that it is a viable form of art, that it is right that it should be put forward and that the development of Impressionism, which interests some people, is a chapter in the history of contemporary art, which it is our duty to display on the walls of our museums. The visitors to the Luxembourg will know, in the fashion of the day, where to give the credit.'

One phase of the Caillebotte affair remains obscure and that is the repeated attempts made later on by Martial Caillebotte to get the twenty-nine rejected pictures accepted by the Nation. According to a letter written in 1928 by Dr. Olivier Merson, in the name of Madame Martial Caillebotte, to Henri Verne, Director of the National Museums, an exhibition was held at Durand-Ruel's during 1908. This was visited by the Director of Fine Arts and by the Curator of the Luxembourg, who was still Léonce Bénédite, and these refused the new offers made by Martial Caillebotte. What opinion can we form of the genuineness of this refusal which we know of only indirectly, from testimony given twenty years after? Their attitude is all the more surprising because fourteen years had gone by since 1894 and because, three years afterwards, the far more 'scandalous' pictures of the Camondo legacy were received without any difficulty *by the Louvre itself*. I have made enquiries at the Durand-Ruel Gallery and can find no trace of any exhibition of this nature in 1908. Without adequate documentation, it is impossible to come to any definite conclusion. In 1928, Monsieur Henri Verne made a last attempt. Is it surprising that it was judged to be somewhat indiscreet?

Sometimes the intensity of a presence is measured by its absence. The dead have right on their side against the living. Two deaths suddenly caused public opinion to veer round. On January 29, 1899, Sisley died in obscurity. Prices of his pictures began to rise slowly in 1897. In the year of his death the prices obtained at the Doria sale (9,000 francs the highest) and at the sale after his death (9,000 francs the highest) accentuated this tendency. In 1904, one of his pictures fetched 40,100 francs in the Bernard sale and Count Isaac de Camondo bought for 43,000 francs at the Tavernier sale in 1900 the *Flood at St-Cloud* which went to the Louvre. Although Gauguin's death in 1903 produced little effect, that of Pissarro who died on November 13 aged 73 had considerable repercussions. All the newspapers celebrated the old pioneer of Impressionism, and the chorus of praise extended all over Europe, to Germany, Austria, England ... Durand-

Ruel's posthumous exhibition of 174 pictures was a triumph.

Thus by the year 1900 public opinion had suddenly changed round. Two events contributed to this: first and especially the exhibition of the thirty-eight pictures of the Caillebotte collection at the Luxembourg which got the public used to this new way of looking at things, and then the Universal Exhibition of 1900. Despite all manner of intrigues, it was impossible to refuse a place to Impressionism there. It was made as inconspicuous as possible. The Impressionists were not allowed in the Decennial Room where the Institut was paramount, which meant that they could show none of their pictures painted after 1890. In the Centennial portion of the Exhibition a room was reserved for them which was much too small. André Mellerio, in a brochure entitled *The 1900 Exhibition and Impressionism*, protested and maintained that there should have been a general exhibition of the whole of Impressionism. (This has, incidentally, never yet been done.) Thus, he said, the precise and definite share of the French School at the end of the nineteenth century would become clear. This had not been only a century of steam and electricity, but also a century of uninterrupted art production, at least so far as painting was concerned. In short, among so many pavilions there was room for an Impressionist Pavilion.

Although it had been very miserly, official France had found room for the Impressionists. The public, encouraged and piqued by curiosity, gathered in crowds and were able to get on familiar terms with the 'monsters'. The Institut did not, however, give in. Gérome, the painter, in a declamatory gesture, tried to prevent the President of the Republic, Monsieur Loubet, entering the Impressionist room, by exclaiming, 'Stop, sir, in there France is dishonoured!'

Meanwhile, the *Olympia,* the dreadful *Olympia,* was in the Louvre. The picture considered to be the most revolutionary of the century was the first to cross the sacred threshold. Monet, the valiant Monet, polished his weapons in 1905 to go to war once more. He wrote to Geffroy: 'Yes certainly it is time to put the administration under the necessity of hanging Manet at the Louvre. We must go at it for all we are worth. If you need further information, don't hesitate to ask me, for there is nothing I would not do for Manet.' Two years later he won his fight. He went and found Clemenceau, at that time President of the Council, who had been his friend for a long time, and he gave the order to hang the famous picture in the Louvre. It is one of my dearest youthful memories to have seen it, before

1924, hanging beside the sacrosanct picture of the Schools, Ingres' *Odalisque,* in the Salle des Etats, a room reserved for the splendours of the Classic and the Romantic movements.

The resistance of the official world to Impressionism expressed itself in 1907 by the refusal of a donation, an event which has been little noticed, except by Gerstle Mack, who mentioned it in his book on Cézanne. In that year, Monsieur Granel, who in 1899 had bought the Jas de Bouffan from Cézanne, offered to the Nation, for the Luxembourg, the murals painted by Cézanne in his youth to decorate the drawing room of the family home. Léonce Bénédite went to Aix-en-Provence to look at them and in a report to the Director of Museums on November 25, 1907, in which he analysed them in detail, he ended by rejecting the gift. 'Granel,' he said, 'offered to detach them from the wall. I dissuaded him, because I am obliged to advise absolutely against accepting this gift. I question neither the talent nor the work of this painter. Is he not represented by other work at the Luxembourg from the Caillebotte legacy? I am careful, therefore, about venturing on this ground, but whatever may be one's feeling for this artist's work, one cannot deny that it would be a singular way of doing him honour to have him represented by flat and banal images which he himself would not appear to have taken seriously!' Doubtless one must be a little more subtle than Mack in order to appreciate Bénédite's decision. For the sake of Cézanne's Impressionist masterpieces, one could reject, at that time, the work he did before 1870. There was no one but Auguste Pellerin to understand it. It is possible to divide these decorations into two parts. One contains those 'images' which include the *Four Seasons,* bought by Ambroise Vollard, the dealer, and bequeathed by him to the Fine Arts Museum of the City of Paris (Petit Palais) where they can be seen to-day. But the rest of this work, *The Magdalen, Christ in Limbo* after Sebastiano del Piombo, and *The Nakedness of Man,* have a romantic force of expression which outdoes the work of Daumier. There is so much interest in them to-day that I was able in 1952 to persuade the Committee of Curators and the Museums Council to buy *The Magdalen,* which had been refused in 1907 by Bénédite.

The curators of museums now began to be anxious about the position created at first at the Luxembourg and then the Louvre by the refusal of the national authorities to buy Impressionist pictures, though the minutes of the Committee of Curators and the Museums Council attest the opposite.

CLAUDE MONET *The bridge at Argenteuil*

On February 1, 1897, Lefenestre, then Curator of the Louvre pictures, suggested to the Council the acquisition of one of Monet's paintings. The reply was that 'the Council forbids in principle the buying from museum funds of work by modern artists' ... this after eight Monets had already come in through the Caillebotte legacy! On January 23, 1899, Léon Bourgeois drew the attention of his colleagues on the Museums Council to the opportunity afforded of buying, at the Boudin exhibition, the *Harbour at Bordeaux* (which did, in fact, reach the Louvre later; see page 105). The Council, however, considered that work by artists recently dead should be bought by the Ministry. Léon Bourgeois did then turn to the Ministry of Fine Arts, for in the same year the latter acquired this picture, Georges Leygues being Minister of Public Instruction. In 1906, twenty-four pictures from the famous collection of the singer Faure were on view and for sale at Durand-Ruel's. The Committee of Curators became agitated, and here is the passage from the minutes of the meeting of March 29, 1906, which

70

reflects their worry: 'At the suggestion of the Director, Monsieur Léonce Bénédite is asked to make an effort to acquire the *Bridge at Argenteuil* by Claude Monet, at present at Durand-Ruel's.' Migeon, André Michel and Leprieur supported this proposal. Léonce Bénédite, while expressing his sincere admiration for certain works of Monet and Manet being shown at Durand-Ruel (at that moment out of the Faure collection), reminded them that, hitherto, no efforts made to persuade the Council had ever come to anything; that it had even decided not to buy the work of any living artist. Nevertheless, in view of this sympathetic demonstration on the part of the Committee, he would approach Messrs. Durand-Ruel and Faure and find out under what terms Monet's *Bridge at Argenteuil* could be acquired. The echo of this affair is heard at the meeting of the Committee of April 5, 1906. 'Although the Council has not expressed itself as being in any way favourably disposed towards the acquisition of a painting by Manet or Claude Monet at present on view at Durand-Ruel, or even to preliminary negotiations, Monsieur Masson informs the Committee that Monsieur Durand-Ruel asks 200,000 francs for the *Bon Bock*, 150,000 francs for Manet's *Jeanne*, and 60,000 francs for the *Bridge at Argenteuil* by Claude Monet. The Committee regrets that the decision of the Council prevents them continuing to negotiate with the possessor of these works.'

The Fine Arts administration did, however, rouse itself, and some very minor purchases were made. But in 1907 it acquired one of Monet's *Cathedrals* (see page 158). In 1910, the Committee of Curators voted for buying a portrait of Théodore de Banville, a pastel by Renoir, for 2,000 francs, 1,000 of which were given by Friends of the Luxembourg. Léon Bonnat firmly maintained the official attitude and did not neglect the opportunity of protesting against the 'favouritism' shown to the Impressionists. At a meeting on January 9, 1905, he called the attention of the Council to the exhibition of works by Monsieur Toulouse-Lautrec at the Luxembourg and regretted that it had been authorised. Monsieur Marcel, Director of Fine Arts who became Director of National Museums in 1913, explained that the matter was outside the jurisdiction of the Council.

It is true that Bonnat knew what he had to deal with in Toulouse-Lautrec, for he had had him as a pupil. He had even said to him, 'You draw abominably', which shows what excellent judgement he had!

In order to get the Council to admit the Impressionists the Curators Committee tried various crafty methods. On December 23, 1914, it received a legacy from Pierre Goujon, a Deputy, killed by the Germans. This legacy included work by two artists particularly loathed by Bonnat, Van Gogh *(The Tea Garden,* see page 228), and Toulouse-Lautrec *(La Toilette,* see page 251). Foreseeing, no doubt, difficulties with the Council, the Committee considered that it would be best to submit them together with pictures by Ribot and Barye, which were included in the legacy. They asked for the pictures to be sent so that the members of the Committee could examine them before the Council meeting. However, this mating of Ribot with Van Gogh did not work. The Barye was accepted for the Louvre and the Ribot for the Luxembourg at the Council meeting of June 7, 1915. It was six months since they had had to consider the legacy of Toulouse-Lautrec and Van Gogh. Here is the relevant passage from the minutes: 'The Council makes reservations, but nevertheless in view of the circumstances of the donation, accepts the legacy for the Louvre.' 'In view of the circumstances.' What circumstances? Apparently one must get oneself killed in battle before one can have a Toulouse-Lautrec or Van Gogh accepted by the Louvre!

But all resistance was overcome by the will of a few great art lovers who had made up their minds to get the Impressionists into the Louvre.

Then began another miracle, the accomplishment of André Mellerio's dream. The finest Impressionist museum in the world was to be started, and the Impressionists, so greatly despised, would have their own pavilion, which would become a sanctuary to which the whole art world would come, and to which young people would make pilgrimages. This miracle was due to the generosity of several representatives of that French middle class which had caused such suffering to these men of genius.

One event at the start of the century affirmed the reconciliation between ancient and modern, that is *peinture claire* artists and their predecessors, Corot and Delacroix. This was the Moreau-Nélaton donation of 1906.

The admiration which Etienne Moreau-Nélaton, a painter and pottery designer himself, had for the nineteenth-century painters was unqualified. Not content with making himself their historian, he gave up what was his whole pleasure for the pleasure of others. On July 27, 1906, by a deed of gift, he gave his collection of pictures to the Nation, on condition that it did not take possession till the time when they could be hung in a place specially designed for them. The Louvre and the Petit Palais of the City of Paris did not make any offers, so Moreau-Nélaton agreed to the works being hung in three rooms given by the Ministry of Finance and the Ministry of Public Instruction in the Louvre building on the Rue de Rivoli side. They were next to the Museum of Decorative Arts and were placed under the care of the Central Union of Decorative Arts. They were ready in 1907.

The original nucleus of the collection had been made by Etienne Moreau-Nélaton's grandfather about 1840. Adolphe Moreau had bought pictures by what was then the avant-garde, Delacroix, Corot, Decamps, Géricault. His son and only child, Adolphe, added little to the collection, but willed the first family donation to the Nation, Delacroix's *Don Juan's Boat,* which thus came into the national collections in 1882. Etienne increased the number of Romantics and added some Impressionists, all within fifteen years. The whole collection, including drawings, amounted to 189 items, valued at 1,580,500 francs. There seem to have been no difficulties over the donation. Was this because, after all, the Louvre building is not the Louvre museum? These rooms were, in some respects, mere anterooms to it. Or did the person of Moreau-Nélaton, greatly respected as he was, prevent argument? The collection did, however, contain Manet's *Picnic,* the 'bomb' of the Salon des Refusés in 1863. But doubtless because the donation was to the French Nation and not to the Louvre, which was not mentioned, the administration of the museums did not feel itself juridically involved. This is how I, at any rate, explain the silence of the minutes of the Consultative Committee and the Museums Council on the subject of this donation, which I only find referred to once, for information, at a meeting of the Council on June 16, 1906, of which the Louvre has not kept the details. The juxtaposition of painters of 1830 and of 1875 in the same collection would have considerable influence on the public taste. Passing from Delacroix to Manet, and still more from Corot to Sisley and Monet, the visitors could appreciate the continuity of the French School, all the more because Moreau-Nélaton had avoided Courbet, whose plebeian power did not appeal to his aristocratic temperament, and because he had chosen Impressionist pictures prior to 1870 or just after, and their subtle atmosphere tied in particularly well with Corot. Sisley, Monet, Berthe Morisot, Pissarro, Fantin-Latour and Manet were the men for his money. Renoir, Van Gogh, Degas, and Cézanne were considered too modern.

Let me add that the pictures shown at the Salon des Indépendants and the Salon d'Automne by the Cubists and Fauves quickly made the Impressionists the representatives of tradition and that it is in their name and in the name of the Nature to which they devoted their art, that the public condemned the new tendencies.

Soon the dykes burst. The Impressionists forced open the doors of the Louvre, some in their lifetime, among them Cézanne whom Manet himself, too middle-class, had been unable to admire. It was the Camondo legacy which accomplished this miracle.

Born of a family of bankers from Constantinople who acquired their title in Italy, Count Isaac de Camondo had collected in his house a complex assemblage of works of art which he had begun to get together about 1890, including some famous Louis XV furniture, made for the Crown, and objects of the eighteenth century, a large series of Japanese prints, pieces from the Far East, and finally a collection of 56 Impressionist paintings as well as some water colours and drawings. Already in 1897, by a deed of gift, he had given to the Louvre some works of art of the Middle Ages and the Renaissance. By his will on December 18, 1908, he left his entire collection to the Louvre with 100,000 francs towards the expense of arranging it. 'The Louvre must take the lot and exhibit them. If this condition is not accepted, I leave my collection to the Petit Palais', he said. In 1911 Camondo died, and the legacy came to the Nation. The Curators Committee met on April 27, 1911, at the Hôtel Camondo, 82 Avenue des Champs Elysées, then adjourned to the Committee Room at the Louvre where they voted *unanimously* for the acceptance of the collection by the Louvre.

These men with all kinds of backgrounds voted unanimously for the entry to the Louvre of seven paintings. On May 8, 1911, the Museums Council reached the same unanimous decision. The minutes, despite the abstract nature of their official style, imply that there were some differences of opinion. The Chairman was still Léon Bonnat. There were some prominent politicians on the Council at that time, who knew French opinion, Léon Bourgeois, who, as Minister of Public Instruction, had accepted *Olympia*, Raymond Poincaré, who in 1912 was President of the Council, and in 1913 President of the Republic, and Georges Leygues, President of the Council after the war. Let the minutes speak for themselves.

Meeting of May 8, 1911

The first item on the agenda was the consideration of the legacy made to the museum by Count Isaac de Camondo. Monsieur Homolle (Director of the National Museums) described the terms of the will.

A discussion started on the question of whether to accept the legacy or not.

Monsieur Bonnat asked if the period of ten years from the death of the artist before a picture could enter the Louvre was fixed in writing or simply by tradition.

Monsieur Homolle replied that he had searched the archives and had found no text imposing a delay of this nature for the admission to the Louvre of contemporary artists. Custom alone has created the tradition.

Monsieur Bonnat remarked that by accepting the Camondo legacy *in toto,* the Council ran the risk of encouraging testamentary donations comprising the works of living artists.

Monsieur Poincaré emphasised the importance of the legacy as an enrichment of the Louvre and advised accepting it. In order to respect tradition and to avoid the danger mentioned by Monsieur Bonnat, he suggested assigning a special part of the Louvre to the collection where it might be exhibited in its entirety.

Monsieur Bourgeois supported this proposal. He thought it was always incumbent on the Council to undertake the arrangements for an important legacy and to reconcile the interests of the Louvre with established usage.

Monsieur Guillemet proposed to give to important collections the far end of the Pavilion de Flore. There the Chauchard, Thomy-Thierry, and Camondo collections could be installed. This part of the Louvre would become the Pavilion of Donors.

The Council proceeded to vote on the question of acceptance.

Monsieur Tétreau proposed the following formula which was put to the vote and passed unanimously:

'The Museums Council, after deliberation, decided unanimously to accept the legacy of Count Isaac de Camondo at the charges and on the conditions laid down by the testator.'

I have often heard people say that the Camondo collection was accepted for its objects of art from older times, and that these helped the modern painting to 'get by'. In the important dossier referring to the donation in the archives of the Louvre, I have found no trace of such a way of looking at things. In the article which he published on the donation in the *Musées de France* (No. 3, 1914) Paul Vitry, at that time joint Curator of the Department of Sculpture of the Middle Ages, the Renaissance, and Modern Times, said, indeed, that it was that part of the collection which was made the centre and which contained certainly the pieces which most attracted the public, but later on he analysed the Impressionist pictures at length and gave high praise to Degas.

Various plans were submitted for the installation of the collection in the Louvre. Leprieur, Curator of Pictures, wanted a complete transference with a regrouping of the nineteenth-century French collections, bequeathed or given by Thomy-Thierry, Chauchard, Moreau-Nélaton, and Camondo, into the first floor of the Pavilion de Flore, which had been given up by the Ministry for the Colonies. The wing of the Tuileries, next to the Pavilion, had already been chosen by Georges Leygues (and chosen in the will which came into effect in 1910) to house the Chauchard collection, which was installed there at the end of 1910, and this was the initial capture of the Pavilion de Flore by the Louvre. But it was only a partial possession, which explains why this first floor was sandwiched in between two floors of offices of the Treasury. It is to be regretted that Leprieur's plan for a Pavilion of Donors was not put into effect, because the work which would have had to be done on the Pavilion would have prevented it being taken back by the Treasury during the 1914 war. This scheme, however, would have meant long delays, and the understandable impatience of Moïse de Camondo, the legatee, to see Count Isaac's collection in its place (for installing it the latter had left 100,000 francs) caused another solution to be adopted. The collection was therefore housed on the second floor of a wing contiguous to the Mollien Pavilion, which had been built by Lefuel. This row of apartments was arranged not like a museum but like a suite of rooms. In order to show the famous set of drawing room furniture, some Louis XV panelling, which the Fine Arts administration had kept when the house of the Military Governor of Paris was demolished in the Place Vendôme, was used. As for the Impressionist pictures, they were hung on every available piece of wall surface in four extremely small rooms.

Out of the 100,000 francs provided by Isaac de Camondo, 19,900 francs were left over from the cost of the installation. This sum the heirs left at the disposal of the museum. The inauguration took place on June 4, 1914, in the presence of the President of the Republic.

The press unreservedly praised the Camondo collection, though it was said in a few papers that the interest of the pictures varied. But the entry of the Impressionists to the Louvre does not appear to have caused a 'scandal'. At this time, anyhow, pictures by these masters still living were fetching large prices. In 1907, the Metropolitan Museum of New York had bought the *Portrait of Madame Charpentier and her Children* for 92,000 francs, but the record price of 435,000 francs was reached in 1912 by the Degas at the Rouart sale which I mentioned above.

What was the attitude of the French provinces during all this debate? Most of the time they said nothing because they knew nothing. Two examples, however, show the provinces more welcoming than Paris. At Lyons, Dr. Raymond Tripier, Chairman of the Museum Commission, persuaded the city to adopt a most fruitful policy with regard to acquiring modern pictures. It bought a *Guitar Player* by Renoir in 1901, followed, before 1914, by pictures by Sisley, Monet, Degas, and even a Gauguin, bought for 39,000 francs. Le Havre showed itself equally up to date when it bought in 1904 two pictures by Pissarro and in 1911, two by Monet, an example which encouraged some useful bequests later on. Béziers was less inspired. There was living there in 1900 a go-ahead man called Gustave Fayet, a collector of Impressionist work, and notably of Gauguin, whose pictures he bought assiduously. Thanks to him, the Béziers Society of Fine Arts organised exhibitions of modern painting. Fayet, Curator of the Museum in 1901, was bold enough to propose to the municipality the purchase of Impressionist pictures. Such was the scandal that he had to resign! Another French town just failed to have a large scale Impressionist museum. Bayonne had seen the formation of Antonin Personnaz's collection. He was a friend of Bonnat, but did not share his taste. A native of those parts, he settled there for good after the 1914 war. He thought of leaving his collection to the museum, but because he considered the locality chosen for it to be exhibited unsafe, he left it to the Louvre.

However, while in France people were arguing over the worth of the Impressionists, they had already won a place of honour in the museums of Germany, and in the big collections in the U.S.A. Russia, too, was already collecting their works.

APOTHEOSIS

ONE of the most curious pages in the history of taste concerns the entry of the Impressionist pictures into the museums of Germany at a time when their merits were so greatly disputed in France itself. It was due to a few pioneers, the first of whom, and the man who gave the impetus to the movement, was Hugo von Tschudi, Director of the National Gallery in Berlin. This gallery filled the same role in Prussia as the Luxembourg in France, being concerned with showing the work of living artists. In 1896, Hugo von Tschudi came to Paris with Max Liebermann, the painter. Both of them were so greatly moved by what they saw at the Durand-Ruel Gallery that Hugo von Tschudi felt impelled immediately to acquire some pictures by these painters for the Berlin gallery. He was clever enough to get these given him by art lovers. His example was soon followed by other big museums. A real competitive spirit seized the German museums to acquire Impressionist pictures, either by purchase or gift. Let me quote a few examples. In 1909, Fritz Wickert supported the donation by a group of art lovers of Manet's *Execution of Maximilian* for Mannheim; from 1909 to 1913, several pictures by Monet, Cézanne, Pissarro, and Sisley were acquired by this gallery. The gallery at Frankfurt-am-Main received a Sisley in 1899. In 1910 it bought Renoir's *Fin du Déjeuner*, in 1912 *Musicians in the Orchestra* by Degas and *Game of Croquet* by Manet. The gallery at Essen acquired, in 1912, the *Sisley and Family* by Renoir, and the *Boats at Anchor* by Van Gogh. The Kunsthalle at Hamburg bought the *Portrait of Henry Rochefort as Hamlet* by Manet in 1907, and the *Portrait of Faure as Hamlet* by the same artist in 1910, in 1913 the *Allée Cavalière* by Renoir, which Alfred Lichtwark had bought, thanks to the enterprise of Gustave Pauli. The Bremen museum began, in 1906, a splendid series of Impressionist pictures by buying the famous *Camille* of the 1866 Salon by Monet. In 1908, the *Portrait of Zacharie Astruc* by Manet and the *Poppy Field* by Van Gogh were added, and in 1911, the *Girl in the Painter's Studio* by Toulouse-Lautrec. The Wallraf-Richartz museum of Cologne bought Van Gogh's *Pont-Levis* in 1911. In 1906, the Stuttgart town gallery received a Monet from the 'Friends of the Stuttgart Gallery Association'. Hugo von

Tschudi's political views caused him to fall foul of the Kaiser. The eminent historian went, therefore, to Munich where he settled down, and started the same movement in respect of the Neue Pinakothek, which became another great centre of Impressionism in Germany. After his death, a veritable avalanche of donations was made in memory of him in 1912 and 1913; four Cézannes, several Van Goghs, Pissarros and Gauguins, thus entered the Pinakothek. This spate of acquisitions was interrupted by the war in 1914 but continued afterwards until brutally interrupted once more, and forbidden, by the Nazis, who obliged the museums to sell some of these 'degenerate' pictures.

The size of this movement presupposes many collectors. German painters themselves bought French pictures, notably Max Liebermann and after him Max Slevogt.

The courageous action of these curators and collectors did not pass unchallenged. Patriotic indignation was added to aesthetic incomprehension, at a time when there was a great deal of tension at the almost certain prospect of the war of 1914. We have said that Hugo von Tschudi fell into disfavour with the Kaiser and had to retire to Munich, where, however, he continued his work with the same zeal.

In 1911, Karl Vinnen, the painter, who was the opposite number in Berlin of Léon Bonnat in Paris, published a *Protest by German Artists,* denouncing the preference given by certain curators of museums to French artists. A group of critics and curators replied, and their arguments were given in a brochure published by Piper of Munich.

The curators replied that their duty was to form collections of European art, and that they must ensure to French art of to-day a place proportionate to the position it enjoyed in contemporary art, a position of considerable importance, not contested by the German artists, since several of the artists who signed Karl Vinnen's protest had undeniably been influenced in their work by French painting. This profession of faith in Europe was the valuable thing about the action undertaken by the curators, critics, and collectors of Germany. It is not irreconcilable with German nationalism, as Meier-Gräfe's attitude showed. In 1902, the latter wrote a book on *Manet and his School,* which was followed in 1903 by *Modern Impressionism,* in 1904 by *The Development of Modern Art,* and in 1907 by *The Impressionists.* He was in Paris during the first years of the century, a popular figure, fêted by the artists in Montmartre and Montparnasse, where there were, in fact, many Germans. He did not, however, hesitate, in 1914, to sign the famous *Manifesto of 93 Intellectuals,* declaring a *Kulturkampf* against French culture.

There is perhaps no stronger proof of the creative force of Impressionism than its astonishing success in Germany. Manet, Monet, Cézanne, and Renoir delivered the painting world from an ambiguity. The combined efforts of all the European schools of painting had set up, between 1750 and 1800, a Neo-Classical aesthetic. The eighteenth century willed it to the nineteenth, but it was completely out of touch with the general development of thought and sensitivity which caused the West to recreate the human conscience in a new way. The artists, restless by nature, were offered as models the art of statuary. In order to express passion with such models, an idealistic aesthetic was suggested to them. Although interested in the Middle Ages, they were forced to mould themselves on the antique.

The whole of this century, so pictorial in spirit, was haunted by sculpture. Neither Gros, Géricault, Delacroix nor Courbet was able to get away from it. At last Impressionism won a belated victory for painting over bas-relief, by analysing optical sensations, and invented a specific language agreeing with the tendencies of the century, expressing itself by colour and feeling, the language of our age.

The reason why the importance of this discovery was felt by certain intelligent men in Germany sooner than in France was because the conception of freedom, which the new school underlined, was far more significant for Germany than for France. Although born of a series of opposing reactions, the four great movements, which displayed, during the course of the century, so remarkable a continuity of creative effort, Neo-Classicism, Romanticism, Realism, and Impressionism, are seen in historical perspective as being in an evolutionary line which, insensibly, leads from fiction to Nature, from thought to feeling, from the ideal to the observed fact. But for Germany, Impressionism represented a break with recent tradition, and a loss of contact with original and deep sources. The freedom which it expressed allowed the native genius of Germany to be reborn in the domain of pictorial expression.

Perhaps because of old traditions which had caused them to excel in drawing, the German School of the last century did not find the example of sculpture a hard one to follow; it was, on the other hand, paralysed by the tyranny of a linear Classicism for which, in 1816, Overbeck and his

HUGO VON TSCHUDI

school took as model the frescoes in the Casa Bartholdy in Rome. To these examples from Italy, used by Overbeck in what the British later called the 'pre-Raphaelite' way, Peter Cornelius and Schnorr von Carolsfeld soon added archaic influences from fifteenth- and sixteenth-century German art. These, however, interpreted according to the letter rather than the spirit, alienated them from, rather than brought them nearer to, expressing the essential German soul, which was glimpsed for a brief moment by a precocious genius, struck down in the flower of his youth, Philipp Otto Runge. Pursuing the aesthetic theories of the Nazarenes, mixed more or less with Biedermeier realism, the historical school of Düsseldorf did not fail to give linearism and mural platitude the same dogmatic and intellectual consequences which were deduced in Lyons and Paris by the school of Ingres. For Germany, Courbet was the first to oppose with the brutal frankness of an artist 'who does not paint angels' the idealism of that school. Preceded with a fair amount of resolution by Leibl and Trübner, Max Liebermann was the true pioneer who, taking Courbet, Manet and Monet in his stride, introduced into Germany, about 1890, the language of liberty. Meanwhile, concurrently with the movement provoked by Impressionism, Edvard Munch, the Norwegian, an astonishing precursor whose position in the hierarchy of European painting is insufficiently recognised outside Germany, was showing the reawakening in all its vehemence of the flow of nordic pathos, while its growing determination to reach the surface was being expressed at the same time by Van Gogh the Dutchman and Ensor the Belgian.

Germany soon adopted Impressionism and made it her own. The revolution caused by the movement born in France engendered across the Rhine another revolution, perhaps even more complete—Expressionism, a magnificent rebirth of the national temperament, in full vigour by 1910, but which was snuffed out by the Nazis in favour of neo-academism.

There is a German artist, Max Slevogt, who incarnates this swing from Impressionism to Expressionism. He owned Manet's *Rue de Berne,* and he changed the peaceful actors painted by Manet in the *Portraït of Faure as Hamlet* into personages full of drama. Lovis Corinth, who was, paradoxically, a pupil of Bouguereau, took one further step and foreshadowed Fauvism. Kirchner in 1906 was at the same stage of evolution as Vlaminck.

Supported by a group of art lovers, artists, and curators, this enthusiastic adoption of 'the way of freedom' was not accomplished without resistance and without causing scandal. Fundamentally, so far as the aesthetic theories upheld in official circles were concerned, the situation for contemporary art movements was not very different in Germany from France. In both countries, the triumph of life over academism was the work of a few exceptional people. Certainly, in 1894, the Caillebotte legacy was only accepted with reservations and was truncated by government circles in France. But two years before, in Berlin, the Association of Berlin Artists, which had invited Munch to hold a special exhibition on its premises, was so horrified by the scandal which this was obviously going to provoke, that they closed it the day after it was opened, ignoring the most elementary rules of hospitality. This event caused the 'Secession', and freed the avant-garde artists from the academic yoke. Bonnat reigned in Paris, but Vinnen laid claim to reigning in Berlin. It was largely through supporting the action of individual collectors that Hugo von Tschudi got the Impressionists into the German museums; in France it was Caillebotte, Moreau-Nélaton, and Count Isaac de Camondo who forced the gates of the museums, preceded by the combative pioneer work of Clemenceau.

The decentralisation of Germany was doubtless a favourable factor on the side of the innovators. The forces of reaction were dispersed in several different centres in different parts of Germany and thus were easier to get the better of. The atmosphere of high tension in which the French art-loving public had lived since the beginning of the century made the opposition to any new movement more violent. Scarcely had the public succeeded in adapting its artistic sensibility to one school of art than it suddenly learnt that the truths so painfully acquired were no longer valid, and that the revolutionary of to-day must be condemned in the name of the revolutionary of yesterday. A resistance only partially defeated by the entry of Delacroix to the Institut, and by the apotheosis of Corot, Millet, and Daumier, about 1875, broke out again in a complex of misunderstandings and rancours, an abscess which burst with the first Impressionist exhibitions.

The quick and intuitive insight into the deeper meaning of Impressionism across the Rhine perhaps fits in with that fermentation of aesthetic ideas at the end of the century to which many German writers bear witness. Thanks to the Germans Semper and Robert Vischer, the Austrians Aloïs Riegl and Strzygowski, and the Swiss Heinrich Wölfflin, it is probable that artistic circles in Germany became more familiar than their opposite numbers in France with certain formal speculations which led them to look for an inner significance in a work of art, and thus enabled them to welcome new ideas with less surprise and shock.

As a result of having preceded by some years their French colleagues in their understanding of Impressionism, the German art historians have perhaps gauged more correctly the extent to which it can be fitted into an historical context. Impressionism appears to the French as above all one of those more authentic demonstrations of their national spirit in its intimate agreement with the exterior world. We like to search for precedents from among our most fundamental traditions. This art of enjoying oneself in pleasant society in natural surroundings we trace stage by stage in the frescoes of Sorgues, the *Très Riches Heures* of the Duc de Berry, the Fontainebleau School, and the eighteenth-century *Assemblies in a Park*. We find Poussin and even Fouquet in Cézanne, while the art of Claude

MAX LIEBERMANN *Self-portrait*

Monet seems to us to have been prefaced by the work of another Claude in the seventeenth century; in Degas we see the heir of Ingres and the Clouets. In a word, it is the expansion of the French genius in all its continuity which it gives us pleasure to recognise in the flowering of talent which came at the end of the last century. What struck the German art historians, on the other hand, was the new and revolutionary character of this movement in the context of European art. This point of view is somewhat paradoxical, since the scandal of this revolution was far less in Germany than in France. The word *Impressionismus* has not quite the same meaning as the word *Impressionnisme*. The French term is an historic idea, the German an aesthetic concept. Less precise, it is, as it were, a dynamic qualification of the idea of modernism. In Germany, not only is there no opposition between Impressionism and twentieth-century movements, but the latter derive naturally from the former. The review *Kunst und Künstler*, directed by Karl Scheffer, on the initiative of the publisher, Bruno Cassirer, became from 1903 onwards a forum for discussion of modern ideas, in which Impressionism was linked to other contemporary movements. In France on the other hand, Fauvism and Cubism ranged themselves just as much against Impressionism as with it, while for some people, not only was Impressionism unworthy of twentieth-century art, but was altogether condemned. Thus it is that for us, Impressionism, thrown out by the Fauves, the Cubists, and the Surrealists, has taken its place among the ancient glories in the history of painting, where it calls to mind forgotten and nostalgic delights. But in Germany, it has kept something of the impetus of its youth.

Impressionism reached the U.S.A. sooner than Germany, but the museums played only a small part. The introduction of modern French art movements was the work of American artists, avid to know what was going on in Paris. Two artists who worked in Paris each had a great deal of influence. Sargent, society painter, although he did not follow the new aesthetic in his work, greatly admired Manet and Monet, and made himself their publicity agent across the Atlantic. Mary Cassatt, who played an active part in the exhibitions of the Impressionist group, was able, because of her easy circumstances and through the important people she knew, to contribute in no small measure to guiding art lovers collecting paintings of 1830–50 (at that time, round about 1870, all the rage in America) in the direction of Impressionism.

If we do not count a touring exhibition of Manet's *Execution of Maximilian,* which only had a *succès d'estime,* the first contact of Americans with Impressionism took place in 1883 at the Foreign Exhibition in Boston, to which Durand-Ruel had sent pictures by Manet, Monet, Sisley, and Boudin. A larger exhibition was held in New York, with the object of collecting funds for the construction of the pedestal of the Statue of Liberty, by Bartholdi, given by France. The 'Pedestal Exhibition' contained work by the Barbizon School, but also some Manets and other Impressionists, thanks to William Meritt Chase (1849–1916), the founder of the Society of American Artists, who was an anti-traditionalist.

In the summer of 1885, James F. Sutton, representing the American Art Association, met Durand-Ruel in Paris and invited him to an exhibition which he was organising in New York. This invitation roused passionate argument among the Impressionists. Monet was hostile to the idea, seeing no future among the Yankees, Renoir was favourable. Durand-Ruel, who had all his expenses paid, and was even excused paying duty except on any pictures sold because of the 'instructive' nature of the exhibition, gave himself up to the preparations for it with the energy of despair, because his affairs were in a bad way. He was proved justified in the event. This large exhibition containing more than 300 works introduced Impressionism to New York in one overwhelming gesture. It opened on April 20, 1886, with 23 Degas, 14 Manets, 48 Monets, 42 Pissarros, 38 Renoirs, 3 Seurats (included at the request of Pissarro), 14 Sisleys, and pictures by Boudin, Cassatt, Caillebotte, Forain, Guillaumin, Berthe Morisot, John Lewis Brown, Roll, and several others. On May 25 it was transported to the National Academy, where its success was even greater. By then some pictures lent by private collectors had been added by A. J. Cassatt, the brother of Mary Cassatt, who was a director of the Pennsylvania Railroad, and Erwin Davis, who in 1881 had bought the *Child with a Sword* and the *Girl with a Parrot* by Manet. These had been bought in Paris by his agent, J. Alden Weir, on the advice of Chase. Mrs. Havemeyer, a friend of Mary Cassatt, who for some years had been buying examples of *peinture claire* on the latter's advice, also lent some pictures.

The Press was divided. The unfavourable notices were, however, very much less virulent than in Paris. The 'revolting' aspect of the pictures was much less apparent to the New York journalists than to the Parisians. Let me quote the paradoxical opinion of the critic of *Amateur Art* who saw in all of them a plagiarising of the old masters: Monet of Turner, Pissarro of Millet, Seurat of primitive Italian frescoes, Manet of Velasquez, naturally. Generally speaking, however, the Press took this demonstration of modern art very seriously. It was welcomed with that cordiality which the Americans always bestow on foreign manifestations in their midst. The fact that it was a commercial undertaking and that the pictures were for sale did not displease them. On the contrary to do business is, in the U.S.A., a good guarantee for the success of any undertaking. The commercial character of any transaction enables it to be taken seriously, and the dealers in works of art are sometimes, in the U.S.A., listened to with more attention than the curators of museums, because they defend the commercial interests of their firms. Durand-Ruel was fêted, and the results of the sale, though not spectacular, were very encouraging: 18,000 dollars on a declared value of 86,320, or almost a quarter. Lovers of *peinture claire* began to vie with one another. By 1890 there were about ten in New York, Albert Spencer, Desmond Fitzgerald, Cyrus J. Lawrence, William H. Fuller, A. W. King-

HENRI MATISSE *Portrait of Stchoukine*

mann, James S. Inglis, A. J. Cassatt, H. C. Havemeyer, who later gave so many fine Manets to the Metropolitan Museum in New York, James F. Sutton, Erwin Davis, who in 1889 gave to the Metropolitan Museum the two Manets which he had bought in Paris in 1881.

At Chicago, Impressionism penetrated to the heart of the World Fair of 1893. The artistic participation of the French Government naturally consisted of academic art, but a private exhibition, entirely from American collections, showed eighteen Impressionist pictures only, which had a great success. The moving spirit behind this exhibition was the famous Mrs. Potter Palmer, who had bought a Monet in 1891 and in 1892 pictures by Pissarro, Sisley, Renoir *(At the Fernando Circus);* she left her fine collection to the Art Institute of Chicago.

In all ages since antiquity, one sign of the success of works of art has been the appearance of fakes. As early as 1889, an article in the *Collector* put American art lovers on guard against cheap imitations of Impressionist pictures.

After the 1914 war, a new generation of art lovers appeared, and then began that competition in prices which has gone on, the prices always rising, till to-day. In 1923, Duncan Phillips bought from Durand-Ruel *The Boating Party* for 125,000 dollars, which makes certain recent prices which have shaken everyone seem not so excessive after all.

The taste of Americans was further stimulated by the large tax rebate obtainable by all who left part of their fortune for the public good, a policy which aims at helping the State in a country where much of the public service is still in private hands. It was therefore inevitable that the finest pictures acquired in Europe should gravitate to the museums, especially Impressionist pictures, which, after giving pleasure to their owners, would rejoice the heart of the public at large.

The Impressionists thus entered America without resistance, as did also modern painting. In 1913 the famous Armory Show, installed in the Armory of the 66th Regiment, showed more than 400 pictures from all the contemporary European schools. Cubism, Fauvism, and later German Expressionism, joined Impressionism in the homes of lovers of art.

As a matter of fact, the creative artist finds the opposite conditions from those confronting him in Europe, especially in France. In Europe, what is new causes scandal. The creative artist requires enormous energy to struggle against the mass inertia of tradition, and to ensure the triumph of 'modern taste' in a generation whose tastes were formed in yesterday's revolution, in process, now, of becoming academic. It is incontestable, however, that this resistance provides a stimulant towards creativeness, for it helps the artist to take the measure of himself. But in the U.S.A., the bias is towards what is new. The country lives in a kind of futurism. In 1900 they were thinking of 1950, and in 1950 of the year 2000. It is therefore not surprising that the reversals of taste which have agitated European opinion so often during the last half century and more have been welcomed in the U.S.A. as being normal demonstrations of 'progress' in the arts.

*

Wars in our time, upsetting by their total character the very bases of civilisation, bring a heightened sense of awareness to the community. They speed up the rate of evolution, and turn what only yesterday was revolution into tradition. After the 1914-18 war France became aware of her real greatness. With a backward glance, made clearer in the light of four years of war, the French realised that the nineteenth century, which the war had just brought to a brutal end, had been, in the domain of art, so extraordinarily prolific that never before, at any period in her history, had France produced such a multitude of geniuses. The Impressionists no longer appeared as revolutionaries, but as the climax of the efforts of this great century, so enamoured of Nature, which modern art comments on so beautifully.

This development of susceptibility had its consequences in the world of the museums, as is shown by the number of works by the Impressionists acquired after the war. But even before it was over, an outstanding artistic event aroused the interest of curators and the Council. This was the beginning of the sale of the contents of Degas' studio. Degas, who was considered to have continued and made his own the tradition of Ingres, died in 1917. He had always been, of all the Impressionists, the one looked on with the greatest favour in official circles, although these always had misgivings about his last period, the most Impressionist of all, which is badly represented in the Louvre. The first sale of the contents of the studio took place at the Georges Petit Gallery in May 1918. The Commission and the Council decided to buy *The Bellelli Family* (page 133), which was acquired for 300,000 francs, 50,000 of which was given by the Count and Countess de Fels, and the *Portrait of Desboutins,* the *Misfortunes of Orleans,* and *Semiramis.* These two last works could, it is true, be suspected of being academic, but there were no doubts of this kind about the *Portrait of Madame Manet on a Couch,* a pastel by Manet, which was bought at the same sale. The Council went so far as to vote 150,000 francs to buy this work, which, however, was considered to be worth only 12,000 francs. In 1919, the Council accepted without opposition the *Portrait of Madame Charpentier* by Renoir, given by the Society of Friends of the Luxembourg. The museums had the benefit at that date of the wise tutelage of Paul Léon, Director of Fine Arts, who favoured the entry of Impressionist pictures to the museums, and thus counterbalanced the influence of Léon Bonnat. He it was who, together with Clemenceau, persuaded Monet to give the eight large panels of the *Water-lilies,* which had already been discussed by the Council on November 8, 1920. The minutes of the Council for the end of

1920 and the beginning of 1921 show his eagerness to acquire the big picture painted in 1866 by the same artist, the *Women in the Garden,* which cost 200,000 francs, a cost shared between the Fine Arts administration and the Réunion des Musées.

The opposition was not, however, completely vanquished. Some acquisitions still caused a scandal. According to a note of Jean Guiffrey's, when the *Portrait of Paul Leclercq* by Toulouse-Lautrec, bequeathed by the sitter, was shown at the meeting of the Council on November 8, 1920, Léon Bonnat, in a fury, exclaimed, 'Well! A nice sort of Louvre you're making for us!' In 1923, the gift of Renoir's *The Bathers* (page 190) by the artist's three sons caused a lot of disturbance. It was the most important work of the Cagnes period that official circles were condemning, using as their excuse that they valued more the work of this artist's Impressionist period! The minutes, brief though they are, bear traces of this battle. 'An argument started and objections were raised by several members of the Council in the name of the tradition which requires the usual interval of ten years to elapse before the exhibition of and entry to the Louvre of pictures by painters recently dead. The acceptance of the picture by Renoir was agreed to' (Meeting of March 5, 1923). The picture only got through, by the way, by one vote (6 to 5). It was said that Renoir's sons had refused 800,000 francs offered them by the American, Barnes, for this picture. At the next meeting, on August 9, 1923, Paul Léon announced that the heirs had agreed that the picture should first be shown at the Luxembourg. Meanwhile a scandal had blown up, which the Press got hold of. There were protests in the curators' department itself, because, contrary to the regulations, the Council had listened to Paul Léon before the picture had been submitted to the Curators Committee. No doubt Paul Léon, alleging that the matter was urgent because of the offers being made from abroad, had hoped to jostle them into a surprise vote, forseeing difficulties, otherwise, in getting the picture accepted. The very same evening as that on which the Council meeting was held, however, d'Estournelles de Constant, Director of the National Museums, met Véra Sergine, Pierre Renoir's wife, at the dress rehearsal of the *War of the Ships,* and was rude to her, regretting that the sons of Renoir had not selected a picture from a period which he considered a better one in the artist's work. Pierre Renoir, whose temper was short, immediately wrote to Paul Léon revoking the gift. But the tact of the Director of Fine Arts arranged the affair and persuaded Pierre Renoir to go back on his decision. It is due to his diplomacy that the Louvre possesses this masterpiece. The letter in which Pierre Renoir revoked his generous gesture ended, none the less, with compliments for the Director of Fine Arts. 'I must now thank you, dear Sir, for having taken up this business in a manner which compels my gratitude. You knew my father, and he esteemed you highly. I shall never forget what you have done, believe me, and above all what you tried to do.' (It was Léon who had recommended Renoir for the Legion of Honour.)

The affair of the *The Bathers* was the outward sign of a new current of resistance, which was now going to attack other painters and another period. Impressionism had been accepted, but now, in its name, they were going to condemn Post-Impressionism.

This term is generally understood, in France, to mean 'Divisionism' or 'Pointillism' as practised by Seurat between 1886 and 1891. But it is better to take the word in its widest sense, as it is understood in Britain, where all that goes beyond Impressionism after 1880 is included. For it was then that there appeared movements which still derived from Impressionism, since they made their effects by means of the principles of pure chromatic technique, and since the point of departure was always the observed fact, but which departed from the essential naturalism of Impressionism, and tended towards Intellectualism (Seurat), Symbolism (Gauguin), and Expressionism (Van Gogh and Toulouse-Lautrec). It is undeniable that French feeling, with exceptions, did not take kindly to these movements, even when their source was the pure Impressionism of Manet and the Argenteuil painters. It is thus easy to understand why, once the revolutionary character of Impressionism had been lost, people saw that in reality it was in complete control of its naturalistic medium. French feeling was less enthusiastic about those who forced the note in representing Nature, and suspected them, not without cause, of having opened the gate to modern aberrations, and included in their disapproval were the 'Constructivist' pictures of Cézanne, and the lyrical Renoirs of the Cagnes period.

This doubtless explains why not a single Cézanne, not a single Van Gogh, and not a single Seurat was bought for the Nation before the second world war. The curators avowed their preference for Degas' works of what I may call his 'Ingres' period, many of which were bought between the two wars. As for Gauguin, he went through a difficult time, even after his death! Robert Rey, a former curator of the Luxembourg, has recalled the arrival of Gauguin's *White Horse* (page 216) at the Luxembourg, and the tumultuous meeting of the Curators Committee on February 7, 1927. 'The members looked at the *White Horse* as if it were going to kick them', he declared. Salomon Reinach spoke quite violently, it appears, against the acquisition, but, according to Robert Rey, there were only three dissenting voices. The picture cost 180,000 francs, 100,000 of which were paid by the museums and 80,000 by the Fine Arts administration.

La Belle Angèle arrived in the same year in most picturesque circumstances. Robert Rey asked Ambroise Vollard to lend it him to show to his pupils at the Ecole du Louvre. Just as he was about to give the picture back to Vollard's chauffeur, the latter handed him a letter from his master saying: 'As the *Belle Angèle* has penetrated into the Louvre, it had better stay there! I shall be quite happy if it does.'

As for Seurat, he got into our museums through the good offices of an American, John Quinn, who bequeathed *The Circus* (page 245) to the French Nation. Quinn had been, about 1910, one of the pioneers of modern art. He was, in New York, one of the organisers of the celebrated Armory Show in 1913. He died in 1925. *The Circus* arrived in France in 1927. After being shown at the Louvre for a brief period, it departed to do penance in the Luxembourg, where it remained until the second world war. It was doubtless with a view to avoiding this fate for his pictures that Jacques Doucet, who died in 1936, formally laid down in his bequest that the *Snake Charmer* by the Douanier Rousseau should be hung in the Louvre, despite the fact that this was contrary to the new regulation which laid down ... and still does ... that a picture may only be hung in the Louvre a century after the birth of the artist. Rousseau was born in 1844.

Meanwhile it was natural that a museum formed by private initiative should have certain gaps, because it reflected the taste of French art lovers, which preferred pure Impressionists to artists who, going beyond that movement, represented modern art. It was these gaps which, after the second world war, Monsieur Huyghe first, and then myself, tried to fill using the feeble resources at our disposal. It seemed, however, a defect which we should never be able to put right, so colossal were the prices asked for works by those artists of whom our epoch is especially enamoured. This gap affected one of the greatest of all, Van Gogh. It was then that the miracle which for fifty years had benefited the Louvre, was renewed by the disinterested generosity of Paul Gachet.

Paul Gachet, the son of the doctor, had witnessed the last hours of Van Gogh. He gave his donation in a way which enabled the curators, overwhelmed by his bounty, to savour to the full the joys of accepting it. Since 1946 he has been a permanent benefactor to the Louvre. In 1949, in memory of his sister, Marguerite, he sent to the Louvre three portraits of the 'Auvers family', a self-portrait by Guillaumin, as well as two splendid works by Van Gogh, the celebrated self-portrait against a background of blue flames, and the effigy of Dr. Gachet. These wonderful gifts were followed two years later by a large batch, including among others, *The Church at Auvers* (page 237) by Van Gogh, three Cézannes, a Renoir, a Monet, two Pissarros, two Guillaumins, and a Sisley. In this way the precious things which Paul Gachet had so carefully guarded in his house at Auvers were transferred bit by bit to a room in the Louvre. He also did not hesitate to give away numerous objects which held memories for him even more precious, perhaps, than the pictures. This donation caused great interest everywhere. A New York paper cabled to the Louvre to ask for the exclusive right to reproduce in colour the *Church at Auvers,* which had not yet been shown. Who would then have imagined that Paul Gachet was about to make another important donation of masterpieces to the Louvre? Six Van Goghs, one a drawing, four Cézannes, three Guillaumins, and a Pissarro arrived at the Louvre from Auvers in 1954. Monsieur Gachet's liberality gave the Louvre eight Van Goghs, or half the total number in the Louvre, which, having once been poor in the work of this master, is now one of the richest, except for some of the Dutch museums.

Despite the difficult times, this example has not failed of its effect and other sons continue the work of their parents in ensuring that the French people have access to the work of their artists. The Louvre had received, in 1929, in a bequest from Monsieur Auguste Pellerin, three of Cézanne's best still-lifes; in 1956, as their share in the celebrations of the fiftieth anniversary of the death of Cézanne, Monsieur and Madame Jean-Victor Pellerin gave unconditionally to the Louvre one of Cézanne's finest portraits, in which he realised in its highest degree that austere classicism which was always his aim, *The Woman with a Coffee Pot* (page 208). This was just the great painting that was needed in order that the Louvre should be able to show the master's art at its most complete.

Jean-Victor Pellerin will not like me talking about him, but I must say that I hope the critics will soon have the chance of once more acclaiming the author of *Tête de Rechange*, which caused such a stir some twenty years ago at the Pigalle Theatre, by the introduction of the technique of parallelism. His father was a remarkable man. All his life he pursued defiantly his vocation of art patron. Starting with Dresden china, he went on to Barbizon and Corot, then sold the lot when he discovered Impressionism. Soon a passion for Manet caused him to jettison everything else. He collected many of Manet's pictures, and his taste was faultless. He bought the *Bar at the Folies Bergères*, the *Monet in a Boat*, and *Breakfast in the Studio*. But then he discovered Cézanne, and that was the final revelation. It was the turn of the Manets to be sold. In 1904 Pellerin bought from Josse Hessel seven pictures by Cézanne, including *The Woman with a Coffee Pot*. In 1906, he lent 25 pictures to the big retrospective exhibition of Cézanne's work at the Salon d'Automne. From now on his predilection did not alter. He stuck to Cézanne and became sufficiently knowledgeable to be able to distinguish the first of his works of the black period. By the end of his life he owned nearly 100 works from every period. Thanks to the loyalty of a family devoted to Cézanne and to the memory of the great art lover from whom they inherited the pictures, nearly all these works are still in France.

Sometimes, a stroke of luck filled one of the places at the Louvre where there was a gap. In 1952 the peace treaty with Japan brought to France the large collection of Prince Matsukata which had been confiscated in Paris, as the property of the subject of a hostile power.*

The wood carvings from Gauguin's hut at Atuana and the celebrated *Breton Village in the Snow* (page 220) were offered in 1952 by Madame Joly-Ségalen with conditions which made it easy to accept the offer. One of the finest of his Tahitian pictures, the *Meal*, dating from 1891, has been given to the Louvre, with the donor Monsieur André Meyer reserving the use of it during his lifetime. Gauguin was for long the poor relation at the Louvre, and had to do penance in the Luxembourg for longer than his colleagues. Now, however, he is very well represented.

* On March 7, 1958, however, the National Assembly voted the restoration to Japan of practically the whole of this collection, containing several hundred pieces, on condition that the Japanese built a suitable museum to house it. This is being designed by Le Corbusier. We have been able to obtain a Van Gogh (p. 227), a Toulouse-Lautrec (p. 245), a Manet, the *Serveuse de Bocks* (p. 125), a Courbet and three Bonvins to supplement the four Gauguin pictures not included in this gift.

To the Gauguins of the Matsukata collection were added Van Gogh's *Vincent's Room at Arles* (page 227), and Manet's *Serveuse de Bocks* (page 125), important for the museum, which has very few works belonging to the *claire* period of this artist. The gaps in the Louvre are, however, being filled in, bit by bit, by art lovers. We received one very fine gift from anonymous donors, Manet's *Beach.*

We owe, too, to Monsieur Laroche, who reserves the usufruct, some splendid pictures, a self-portrait by Cézanne, a Toulouse-Lautrec, a Monet, Renoir's great red-chalk drawing, *Bathers,* a self-portrait by Van Gogh, and a head by Corot. I must here mention Dr. Charpentier, whose marvels I have often looked at in his house in the Boulevard Haussmann, where the doctor, whose original tastes included a passion for Boucher, did the honours in which he promised that the Louvre should one day have its share, to the tune of eight paintings and one pastel drawing. The last of these generous bequests to the Louvre was the gift of part of Monet's *Picnic* (page 148) by Georges Wildenstein (a picture which, as we have seen, was of the highest importance in the story of Impressionism), that of Manet's charming *Asparagus* by Sam Salz of New York and the bequest by Madame Frédéric Lung of Algiers. Madame Lung, who at first had intended it for the Algiers museum, finally gave it to the French State, as a result of political developments in Algeria. The Musée de l'Art Moderne also benefited from the bequest; in 1960 the Louvre received three Renoirs, an admirable Gauguin, *Arearea,* also called *The Red Dog* and the *Argenteuil* of 1872, one of the artist's most spontaneous works.

The miracle of Impressionism is inexhaustible. There was a magnificent collection in Paris containing both Impressionist and contemporary art; it had been built up by Paul Guillaume, an avant-garde dealer whose death caused much dismay among artists. As an art critic writing in defence of the painting then being done in Paris, I was in close touch with Paul Guillaume; after the second world war, I continued to enjoy the friendship of his wife, who after his death married the architect Jean Walter, Monsieur and Madame Jean Walter carried on Paul Guillaume's work, adding some fine pictures to the collection; they often expressed a wish to me that the public should benefit from this unique ensemble. After the sudden death of Jean Walter, the transfer of the collection to the state was finally achieved, thanks to the efforts of Madame Jean Walter, who overcame every obstacle, and through the mediation of the Société des Amis du Louvre; it took the form

VINCENT VAN GOGH *Portrait of Doctor Gachet*

of a 'Paul Guillaume-Jean Walter Foundation', and was exhibited in 1966 in specially constructed quarters on the Terrasse des Tuileries, opposite the Jeu de Paume. Madame Jean Walter, who has retained the usufruct of her collection, contributed to the cost of the building.

Thus, gift by gift, picture by picture, the Impressionist Museum took shape. Completed by acquisitions made because of their bearing on some important point, sometimes obtained by luck, it gradually became a balanced collection, truly representative of this great French movement.

The situation after the 1914 war was that the pictures were housed partly in the Louvre (Camondo collection) partly in the Museum of Decorative Arts (Moreau-Nélaton collection) partly in the Luxembourg (Caillebotte collection and purchases by the State). The set-up at the Luxembourg was unsatisfactory. It had for long objected to the Impressionists, and was not, therefore, likely to welcome the Fauves, the Cubists, and the Surrealists. The proximity of Bouguereau, Cabanel, Gervex, Cormon, Latouche and

96

the like to the painters whose works were the glory of French art seemed most regrettable. It was decided, therefore, to move them to the Orangery of the Tuileries. This was going to house Monet's *Water-lilies,* which arrived there in 1927.

In 1924, therefore, Léon Bénédite declared that 'the oranges must give place to the pictures'. This arrangement seemed all the more sensible because the pictures by foreign artists had been moved to the Jeu de Paume, a building similar to the Orangery, on the opposite corner to the Tuileries terrace. This effort to form a gallery of modern artists not French was so badly thought out that to-day there is scarcely anything left of it. Bénédite did, indeed, spend a lot of money on it, but his taste had more disastrous consequences for this collection than for the Gallery of Modern French Art. (He even considered pictures by Constantin Meunier, Alfred Stevens, Henri de Braekeler, Baertson and Claus to be 'undoubted masterpieces worthy of the Louvre'.)

The idea of moving the Impressionist pictures to the Orangery of the Tuileries was, however, given up, doubtless because it was feared that the public would think it an excuse to be rid of them on the part of the Louvre authorities. It was therefore to the Louvre that Henri Verne, Director of the National Museums in 1925, proposed to move the Caillebotte collection and other Impressionist pictures from the Luxembourg, with only a few works, such as Cabanel's *Venus,* representing official art. The Under-Secretary of State of the time, André François-Poncet, welcomed this suggestion with enthusiasm and managed to get it carried out. A room was specially arranged on the top floor of the Colonnade, in 1927. A little later the Moreau-Nélaton collection was moved from the Museum of Decorative Arts to the Louvre and once there to the rooms adjoining those housing the Caillebotte collection. This was in 1934. A few Impressionist pictures remained for some time at the Luxembourg, as examples of what the authorities persisted in calling 'modern art'. *The Circus* by Seurat was imprisoned there until the second world war.

Part of the Impressionist collection was rehung in a wing of the Colonnade, but a long way from that other important group, the Camondo collection. After the second world war, it was obvious that, even allowing for the Pavillon de Flore, the available premises within the Louvre would be insufficiently large to house all the collections of the Picture Department. Also, among the masterpieces of which it had been deprived for four years, the public was especially anxious to see once more the Impressionist pictures. To take over the premises in the Louvre would have meant long and expensive work arranging them, but the Jeu de Paume, abandoned by the department recovering works of art from the Nazis, was available. There was no question of reopening it, for it contained few and poor specimens among its works of art. Georges Salles, who became Director of the National Museums in 1945, therefore adopted the proposal of the Picture Department, and decided to turn the Jeu de Paume into an Impressionist Museum which, for the first time, would reveal the astounding richness of our collections in a setting better suited to their character than the austere walls of the Louvre. From the rooms the visitors could see the changing colour of the Parisian sky so often painted by these artists, and the miniature regattas on the Tuileries ponds would help them to recall those of Argenteuil. The museum would become, in Georges Salles' words, 'the Louvre's country cottage'.

We found the heirs of the great donors most understanding. Once more we realised that these fine Frenchmen had worked for the triumph of their favourite artists, and had not thought of themselves. And so this museum, unique the world over, came into being.

I had the joy, in the spring of 1947, of preparing for the opening of this marvellous museum, which was to be one of the great post-war attractions of Paris. During the war, and even just after the liberation, the charms of the Impressionists might seem old fashioned. That gracefulness, that femininity, did not suit an age of iron. In the warehouses in which they were stored, such quantities of masterpieces, arranged like books on shelves, did not, Impressionist though they were, appeal to our feelings. We liked everything that gave us confidence in French energy: Géricault, David, Delacroix, Fouquet, Georges de la Tour, and that *Pietà* from Avignon which we venerated as the symbol of a France down, but not out.

In 1947, the inauguration of the Impressionist Museum, which almost coincided with the second anniversary of the Allied victory, seemed a kind of symbol of peace, whereas the tragic art of Picasso, Rouault and Soutine had foretold the time of horror. Impressionism gave back to us the vision of the days when life was agreeable, back in the nineteenth century, when Man, as always when his soul is at peace, paid court to Nature.

The building of the Jeu de Paume, constructed out of light materials without foundations, was soon seen to be a most unsuitable place in which

98

to house the fragile Impressionist works. At my request, in November 1954, Georges Salles ordered it to be closed, prior to a complete renovation.

The chief architects, Jean-Charles Moreux, Lahalle, and myself studied with the greatest care how to transform this building, so that it would conform to all the exacting requirements of a modern museum, as regards lighting, natural and artificial, air conditioning, visibility of the pictures, and drying out the building, which was permeated by damp.

During the reconstruction of the Jeu de Paume, the paintings were put in the hands of the restoration department of the Louvre so that the varnish could be lightened; in some cases, this had discoloured and was affecting the colour balance. In addition, the framing of the pictures was completely over-hauled. The majority were still in the hideous rococo-type frames which were fashionable when they were being painted; to save money, they had been gilded with artificial gold, which had blackened unpleasantly in the course of the years. The re-framing was done in several ways; some works, in particular those of Renoir and Cézanne, were best displayed in antique frames, while others were shown to advantage in the type of channelled frame finished in gold leaf which has been in use from the nineteenth century to 1970. Finally, for many of the other pictures I broke new ground by having modern frames made, without any carved decoration, of mahogany, ash, maple or sycamore. In so doing, I was acting upon suggestions made by some of the Impressionists themselves (Pissarro, Gauguin and Degas, for example) regarding the type of frame they would have preferred.

On June 10, 1958, this brand-new museum had the honour of being in-augurated by Monsieur René Coty, President of France. Borrowing the words of Gérome to President Loubet at the inauguration of the Impressionist section of the universal exhibition of 1900, I remarked to President Coty: 'Monsieur le Président, this museum is the glory of France'.

✴

The reputation of this style of painting has not evaporated. It still strongly affects young people. The variations in taste seem to have passed it by. One would have thought that enthusiasm for abstract art would make the present generation insensitive to the Impressionists. This has not happened. In the U.S.A. both abstract and Impressionist art are practised and the latter is extremely popular. It is possible that this popu-larity is due to the taste for the abstract, being explained by a kind of nostalgia, only half realised perhaps, for that Nature with which people to-day have lost contact, and of which Impressionism offers an interpretation which for them is viable because modern. The profane, entirely lay character of this style of painting also perhaps helps its success. Monet remains for us 'the young man who does not paint angels', as Courbet called him, and more so than Courbet himself, who painted at least one religious picture.

Impressionist humanism is a really up-to-date humanism, the sort of which Baudelaire dreamed. It shows humanity delivered from its ancient obsessions, both with religion and history, as well as metaphysics. In the morning of the world, Man goes forward joyfully, with a smile on his face, drawn by the light. Impressionism is the reflection in art of that philosophic attitude of the nineteenth century which trusted that humanity would be freed from its servitudes, and in a fit state, therefore, to ensure happiness and goodness for everyone. Cézanne tried to give a classical and therefore solid base to this hedonistic viewpoint, while Renoir, during the Cagnes period, clothed it in the forms of primal innocence, and Seurat, in the few years that were allowed him, remembered the words of Goethe, 'Stop, you are so beautiful!' and pinned down the passing moment, and made it eternal. Tormented by the mirage of far-off countries, Gauguin nevertheless was not deflected from the hedonistic Impressionist ideal. He searched for deeper foundations for that trust between man and man which should exist, thinking to find it in the so-called pure and primitive races of the South Seas. With Van Gogh it was a case of too much loving. His spasms are like the ecstasies of the mystics, rather than the convulsions of the Romantics. Pessimism appeared with Toulouse-Lautrec, who thus heralded our times.

From Spain rose up a prophet who spoke to humanity in quite another language. Cézanne and Renoir were still alive when Picasso, in his Blue Period, depicted a wretched and emaciated humanity, resembling that which emerged from the concentration camps forty years later. Life is just as dramatic as art. Beyond those forty years when mankind was a prey to the horrors of both peace and war, we look back, so as to renew our confidence in ourselves, to that epoch when a painter could produce a masterpiece from a wisp of cloud, the winding of a stream, the smoke of a locomotive in a railway station, the rustle of a silken dress, a girl's smile.

MAURICE DENIS *Homage to Cézanne* (detail)

Impressionism is not yet ready to be put on the shelf, as the art of Raphael, for instance, was for four centuries. Their own kind of magic ensures that the work of the painters who lived between 1860 and 1920 remains, for us to-day, a never ending source of happiness and delight.

THE PLATES

JOHANN BARTHOLD JONGKIND, 1819–1891

The Castle of Rosemont

EUGÈNE BOUDIN, 1824–1898

The Harbour at Bordeaux. Signed and dated 1874
Canvas: 28⅝ × 40⅛ in. (70 × 102 cm.) Cat. R.F 2716

Acquired by the State in 1899

The war of 1870–71 dispersed the Impressionist painters, who took refuge either in England or in Belgium. Boudin chose the latter; during the summer of 1871 he spent six weeks in Antwerp, and thus had an opportunity of seeing a large sea-port, whereas previously he had only visited the little fishing-ports of Normandy and Brittany. The grey fog of Antwerp presented him with an atmosphere very different from the moist luminous skies he had studied in the Seine estuary, and in the Flemish port he painted some

landscapes with skies of more ashen tones. When he returned to Paris, he took part from 1874 onwards in the exhibitions organised by his Impressionist friends; but although he had initiated their movement, he did not follow them in their more revolutionary innovations. For this reason he did not fall into such disfavour with the public, and was more easily able to find patrons. At this time he was fifty years old, and at the height of his powers. He divided his time between Trouville, Brittany and Paris; but occasionally undertook longer journeys to Bordeaux (1874), Rotterdam (1876), Dordrecht (1884) and again to Bordeaux (1889).

The Harbour at Bordeaux, which he painted in 1874, is a somewhat exceptional work, first of all because of its size. His pictures are usually paintings of atmosphere; here, however, he has set himself to depict the life of a great port, with its forest of masts and the busy disarray of the quays with their wagons and carts. A cloudy, leaden sky, somewhat rare in Boudin's work, serves to emphasise the oppressive effect of exhausting labour.

The Jetty at Deauville. Signed and dated 1869
Canvas: 9 × 12¹/₂ in. (23.5 × 32.5 cm.) Cat. r.f. 1967

In the Auguste Rousseau collection; bought from him for 1,575 francs in the sale of March 9, 1900, by Count Isaac de Camondo, and bequeathed by him to the Louvre in 1908; in the Louvre in 1911; shown in 1914.

Boudin was born at Honfleur and died at Deauville. All his life and work were dominated by the Seine estuary, the source of the open-air school and of Impressionism. This Norman was the son of a former naval gunner, who at that time sailed between Honfleur and Le Havre. In 1845, Millet started him off on his vocation. Boudin sent in some work to the Society of the Friends of Art of Le Havre. His contribution was noticed and brought him a municipal grant and he went to Paris to study for three years. But he preferred painting seascapes of Normandy from life.

In 1859 Courbet, passing through Le Havre, discovered in a shop window some small landscapes painted on shovelboards. He got himself introduced to their author, and together they went to lodge with 'Mother' Toutain, whose inn, called the 'Ferme Saint-Siméon', overlooked the Seine estuary, and was a rendezvous for artists. In the district they met Baudelaire who invited them to the house of his mother, the widow of General Aupick.

It was shortly before this encounter that Boudin 'discovered' Claude Monet who was showing some caricatures in a stationer's shop. Monet said later: 'It is owing to Eugène Boudin that I became a painter.'

In 1861 in Paris, he got to know Corot, who dubbed him later 'the king of skies'; in 1862 he met Jongkind at Honfleur. He spent his time thence-

The Port of Antwerp   *Sailing Boats*

forth partly in Normandy, and partly in Brittany and Paris. For several summers he painted on the fashionable beaches of Deauville and Trouville.

The Jetty at Deauville does indeed show several people, but no longer in worldly and leisurely meetings on a sandy beach in the sunshine. These few persons are an the jetty to watch the movement of the boats, the white sails of which can be seen near the lighthouse at the end of the jetty. The whole of the foreground consists of an almost entirely empty space. Two-thirds of the canvas are kept for the sky, Boudin's favourite subject.

PAUL-CAMILLE GUIGOU, 1834–1871

The La Gineste Road

The Laundress

HENRI FANTIN-LATOUR, 1836–1904

Narcissi and Tulips *Study of a Nude Woman* *Still-life with Flowers and*

The Edge of the Forest   *The Pink Dress*

Family Reunion. Signed and dated 1867
Canvas: 60 × 91¹/₂ in. (152 × 232 cm.) Cat. R.F. 2749

Shown at the Salon in 1868; retouched in 1869; in the collection of
Marc Bazille, the artist's brother; in the Luxembourg in 1905, by agreement
with Monsieur Marc Bazille; transferred to the Louvre in 1929.

The credit of having invented open-air portraiture belongs to Bazille
and Monet. After 1865, Bazille painted the *Pink Dress,* and Monet painted
his *Picnic* (see page 148) at Chailly. These two works, however, though
begun in the open air, were finished in the studio. The *Family Reunion* in
1867 was, apart from a little retouching, painted entirely out-of-doors.

During the summer of 1867, Bazille set up his easel beneath the big
chestnut tree on the terrace. From there he overlooked the picturesque village
of Castelnau, separated from Méric by a ravine in which flows the Lez. All
the members of his family are shown here. In the foreground, sitting on a
bench, are his father and mother; at the back, the eldest of his cousins and
her husband Monsieur Teulon; at the round table, Madame des Hours,
Bazille's maternal aunt, with her daughter Thérèse; sitting on the parapet
of the terrace, Camille des Hours, his youngest cousin, beside the young

Marc Bazille; on the extreme left, standing, his uncle des Hours, behind whom can be seen, half-hidden, the tall silhouette of the artist.

Motionless and gazing directly at the artist, these people give the impression of posing for a photograph. They are out-of-doors but this has not prevented them from keeping to a rather stiff pose, of the kind often taken up by a model in an art school. The likenesses, which one feels are very good, increase this impression. How different they are from Monet's *Women in the Garden,* who are silhouettes in a natural setting rather than portraits. Perhaps the Protestant origin of the Bazille family partly accounts for this dignity, austerity, and self-sufficiency.

Bazille did, however, retouch this big picture in a few places, for the following winter he wrote from Paris to his parents: 'I shall send the Méric picture to the exhibition. I have retouched it. I have put in some little dogs and redone the heads of Pauline and Camille which I didn't like. I have begun this and shall finish in a month's time.' He changed some more, in fact, replacing the little dogs by a still-life in the foreground; flowers, a hat and an umbrella, beside luminous patches of sunshine.

EDOUARD MANET, 1832–1883

Lola de Valence. Signed and painted in 1861–1862
Canvas: 25¹/₂ × 32 in. (123 × 92 cm.) Cat. R.F. 1991

Valued by Manet himself in 1871 at 5,000 francs (listed in his memorandum book) this picture was sold for only 2,500 francs by the artist to

Faure, the singer, in 1873; Faure sold it to Camentron the merchant, between 1890 and 1893; it was acquired by 'Father' Martin, a picture dealer, and bought from him for only 1,500 francs by the Count de Camondo in 1893; he bequeathed it to the Louvre in 1911 and it was exhibited in 1914.

Manet discovered the principles of his revolutionary style of painting chiefly in Spanish art. He visited in his youth the fine Spanish collection which Louis-Philippe had assembled in the Louvre and which he took back in 1848. What has been overlooked, however, is that Manet may have rediscovered Velasquez later on during a trip to Vienna in 1853. But Goya is obviously at the back of this picture, inspired by the star dancer of a ballet troupe which had come from Madrid in the autumn of 1862. On days when they were not dancing, artists of the troupe used to come and pose in the studio which Manet's friend Stevens had lent him, his own being too far from the Hippodrome where the troupe was performing.

After painting a scene from the ballet *Flor de Sevilla*, which he called *Spanish Ballet* (Phillips Memorial Gallery, Washington), Manet invited Lola de Valencia, the star of the troupe, to pose alone. He depicted her in the wings, framed by the structures carrying the 'flats'.

The painter's friends considered this picture, which they saw when it was still in the studio, highly successful. Baudelaire admired it and wrote a quatrain on the subject.

A short while afterwards, this portrait was shown at the Martinet Gallery on the Boulevard des Italiens, where both the criticism and the praise it received did much to spread the fame of the artist.

Moonlight. Harbour at Boulogne

Still-life with Fruit

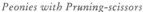

Peonies with Pruning-scissors   *Angélina*

Le Déjeuner sur l'herbe (The Picnic). Signed and dated 1863
Canvas: 84 × 106 in. (214 × 270 cm.) Cat. R.F. 1668

This picture was refused by the Salon in 1863 and shown at the Rejects
exhibition of the same year under the name of *Le Bain (The Bathe)*; in the
list he made in 1871 of his work, Manet called it *La Partie Carrée (The
Foursome)* and valued it at 25,000 francs; it was bought by Faure the
singer in 1878 for 3,000 francs together with two youthful works (copies
of pictures by Velasquez and Filippino Lippi); Faure sold it to Durand-Ruel,
the dealer, in 1898 for 20,000 francs, from whom Etienne Moreau-Nélaton
bought it for 55,000 francs; it was given by him to the Nation in 1906; in
1907 it was on view at the Museum of Decorative Arts (together with the
whole of the Moreau collection) and came to the Louvre in 1934.

Napoleon III called this picture 'indecent'. It caused an enormous
scandal at the Rejects exhibition. The models were Victorine Meurend,
Gustave Manet, the artist's brother, and Léon Koella-Leenhoff, the son of
his future wife, who was taken to be her younger brother.

An astute British critic, Hamerton, who wrote for a London periodical,
saw in this picture 'a transposition into terms of the France of to-day of
an idea of Giorgione.' Manet later admitted to Antonin Proust that he had
copied Giorgione's *Concert Champêtre* in the Louvre and that he wished
to produce a new version of it. In the year 1864, however, the critic Ernest
Cheneau had discovered the true origin of the picture in Raphael's
Judgment of Paris, known only through a drawing and two engravings by

Marcantonio and Marco Dente. But this discovery passed unnoticed. Manet took great care not to reveal the source of his inspiration. It was Gustav Pauli who, in 1908, let it be known that Manet had simply copied the positions of the three figures placed on the right-hand side of Marcantonio's engraving. Thus the Salon rejected a composition by Manet which was inspired by the master most revered in the schools. Manet may also have known this same composition as it appeared in the Hofburg in Vienna, in a tapestry based on a cartoon by Coypel the Elder, for he was in Austria in 1853. Raphael himself took ideas from antique sarcophagi.

The Fifer

This painting was acquired by the Louvre with the Isaac de Camondo bequest (1911). It had been rejected by the Salon of 1866, and this provoked a lively reaction on the part of Emile Zola; in his review of the Salon in *L'Evénement,* he gave high praise to the artist. The simplification of planes and colours is inspired by Velasquez, whose work Manet had studied at the Prado in 1865. The model was probably an 'enfant de troupe' (a child born and brought up in barracks). Manet's pupil, Eva Gonzalès, was inspired by this picture in her own painting of *Un enfant de troupe,* now in the museum of Villeneuve-sur-Lot.

Olympia. Signed and dated 1863
Canvas: 51 × 74³/₄ in. (130 × 190 cm.) Cat. r.f. 644

Exhibited at the Salon in 1865, then at the Universal Exhibition of 1867, and in Manet's hut; it was in the Manet sale, February 4 and 5, 1884, after his death (No. 1); it was withdrawn from the sale by Madame Manet and offered to the Nation by public subscription organised in 1889–90 through the initiative of Claude Monet, price 19,415 francs; it became part of the Luxembourg collection in 1890, and was transferred to the Louvre in 1907 on Clemenceau's orders instigated by Monet.

In the Salon of 1865 Manet showed a nude which he had painted in 1863 with Victorine Meurend as the model. She was shown lying on a bed with a cat, while a negress offered her a bouquet. Fearing, perhaps, that another 'Rejects exhibition' would be organised, the judges accepted Manet's contribution. This unidealised nude, as well as the equivocal presence of the negress and the cat, caused a scandal, and abuses were showered upon the 'Venus with cat', 'Odalisque with a yellow stomach', 'Female gorilla'. 'Crowds surrounded the decaying flesh of Monsieur Manet's

115

Olympia. When art reaches so low a level it is not worth condemning,' so Théophile Gautier and Edmond About pronounced in chorus. The disconcerted judges had the picture 'sky-ed', so that it could not be seen.

Manet, a sensitive and highly emotional person, shattered by such a reception, wrote to Baudelaire of his disillusionment. The latter, excellent critic as he was, tried, in his reply, to restore Manet's flagging spirits. 'Do you consider yourself a greater genius than Chateaubriand or Wagner? Everyone made fun of them, and they survive.' When the Salon closed, Manet decided to calm himself down by taking a short trip to Spain.

Two years later, on the occasion of the Universal Exhibition of 1867, Manet, at the suggestion of Courbet, had a private hut built on the Avenue de l'Alma, where he showed his pictures by themselves. He kept this canvas till his death, and considered it his masterpiece. It has been said that this picture was inspired by Goya; it may derive from Goya in spirit, but the pose is taken from Titian's *Venus of Urbino*.

Finally, in 1907, at the instigation of Claude Monet, Clemenceau ordered Manet's *Olympia* to be transferred to the Louvre.

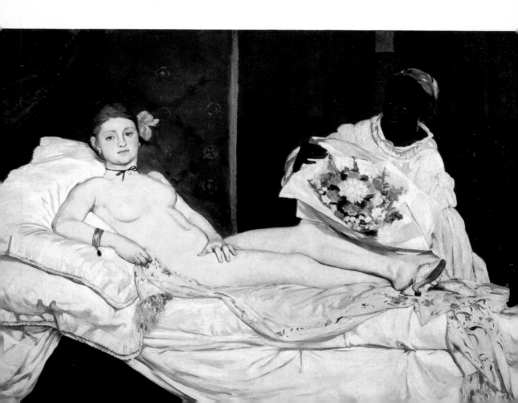

Peonies. Signed and painted about 1864–1865
Canvas: 36⅝ × 27⅝ in. (93 × 70 cm.) Cat. R.F. 1669

Durand-Ruel paid Manet 400 francs for this picture in 1872 and sold
it to John Saulnier of Bordeaux for 600 francs; he bought it back again at
the Saulnier sale, June 5, 1886, for 680 francs and sold it to Etienne
Moreau-Nélaton, who gave it to the Nation in 1906; it was on view with
the whole of the Moreau collection in the Museum of Decorative Arts in

1907; in 1934 it was exhibited in the Louvre.

Etienne Moreau-Nélaton wrongly thought that this was the picture given by Manet to his friend Thoré as a thanks offering for a eulogistic article, but this was another picture which reached the Louvre in 1914 as part of the Camondo donation (page 113).

Flowers played a great part in the development of Impressionism. The artists used them as experimental fields in their studies of colour. Manet began to paint vases of flowers in 1864 and continued to do so till his death.

Those pictures on view before 1870 at Cadart's or Martinet's, such as his still-lifes, were better understood by the critics than his other compositions.

Flowers often enhanced Manet's pictures, apart from canvases devoted entirely to them, for instance in pictures such as the *Picnic* (page 114), *Blonde with Bare Breasts* (page 126), *Olympia* (page 116), and the *Portrait of Zola* (page 119).

Peonies seem to have been Manet's favourite flower. He grew them in his garden at Gennevilliers and painted as many as fifteen pictures of them. The variety which he has painted both in this picture and in the others is 'paeonia sinensis', which had been introduced from China at the beginning of the nineteenth century. The fashion for it, during the second half of the century, coincides with a revival of Far Eastern influences which affected painting at this time. The peony was part of the sumptuous decoration of the salons of the Second Empire. It was in 1787 that a doctor of the East India Company, named Duncan, succeeded in procuring a specimen of this flower which he gave to Kew gardens. The peony was one of the favourite flowers of the Chinese and Japanese.

Portrait of Emile Zola. Painted in 1868
Canvas: 57$^1/_8$ × 44$^7/_8$ in. (145 × 114 cm.) Cat. R.F. 2205

Given by Manet to Zola; given by Madame Zola to the Louvre in 1918, Madame Manet retaining meanwhile the usufruct; it became part of the Louvre collection in 1925.

It was after the rejection of Manet's *Fifer* by the judges that the 'Manet scandal' had further repercussions. Zola was commissioned by Monsieur de Villemessant, managing director of the *Evénement,* to write a series of articles on the Salon. His violent articles, signed 'Claude', were prophetic.

'We laugh at Monsieur Manet,' he wrote, 'but our children will go into raptures before his pictures. I have a good mind to predict that this will happen very soon. I am so positive that Manet will be one of the masters of tomorrow that I should consider I had done a good stroke of business to-day if I had the money and bought all his pictures. In ten years they will be selling for fifteen, twenty times the price.'

These articles were brought together by Zola in a brochure entitled *My Salon* (later incorporated in a selection entitled *My Hates)*. They caused a rain of protests to descend on the *Evénement,* as well as the cancellation of a good many subscriptions. The managing director, in an attempt to calm public opinion, added to the staff of critics a more conventional colleague, who proceeded to praise all that Zola criticised. The latter refused to play, and resigned. In 1867 a more profound study of Manet's art appeared in the *Revue du XIXème Siècle* under Zola's signature, consisting of twenty-three pages headed: *A new way of painting: Monsieur Edouard Manet.* Manet in gratitude offered to paint Zola's portrait. Zola sat for it at the artist's home in the Rue Guyot, from November 1867 to February 1868. For the setting, however, Manet drew on the workroom of the novelist. The accessories in the picture, like the principal features, were a manifesto of the new school of painting: the Japanese screen, the Utamaro print recalling the influence of the Japanese prints, the engraving of Velasquez's *Topers* and beside it an engraving of Manet's own *Olympia.* The title of Zola's brochure serves as signature.

The portrait was sent to the 1868 Salon, and admitted by the judges but hung very high up between two doors. It received malevolent and venomous criticisms to which the artist was by now becoming inured.

Lady with a Fan   *Lady with Fans*

Madame Manet on a Blue Sofa   *Reading*

The Balcony. Signed and painted in 1868–1869
Canvas: 65 × 49¹/₄ in. (169 × 125 cm.) Cat. R.F. 2772

This picture was exhibited at the Salon of 1869; the painter Caillebotte bought it for 3,000 francs at the sale of Manet's studio in February 1884; he bequeathed it to the Luxembourg in 1896 and it went to the Louvre in 1929.

At Boulogne where Manet was staying with his family in 1868, the idea came to him to paint a picture of a balcony with people in a room seen from outside. It was the strange contrasts of light which induced him to make the attempt, which was carried out in Paris. Berthe Morisot was one model. She is sitting on a stool on the left of the picture. Standing near her is Jenny Claus, who later married a friend of Manet, the painter Prins. Standing between the two of them is the painter Guillemet. The model for the young boy in the shadows at the back carrying a dish filled with food was Léon Koella-Leenhoff, Madame Edouard Manet's son, who passed for her younger brother.

Manet had made a first sketch for *The Balcony* at Boulogne, in which Mademoiselle Claus occupies the place later filled by Berthe Morisot.

This very curious picture, partly inspired by the *Manolas* of Goya, was accepted by the 1869 Salon. Berthe Morisot wrote about the private view to her sister: 'I found Manet with his hat on the back of his head and looking demented. He begged me to go and see his picture because he did

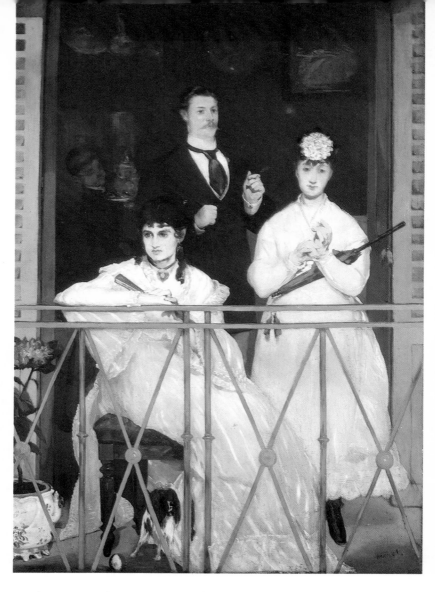

not dare to do so himself. He laughed, looked worried, swearing all the time both that the *Balcony* was a very bad picture and that it would be very successful.' She herself seemed pleased with her portraits, for she added:

'I appear strange rather than ugly. It seems that those looking at me have murmured the words "Femme fatale".'

The critics, however, were hard. Berthe Morisot wrote: 'Poor Manet is sad. His exhibits are, as usual, not to the taste of the public — a perpetual source of surprise to him.'

The *Balcony* remained in Manet's studio till his death.

Portrait of Mallarmé. Signed and dated 1876
Canvas: 10¼ × 13½ in. (26 × 34 cm.) Cat. R.F. 2661

In Mallarmé's collection; then in Madame Mallarmé's; then in that of Dr. Edmond Bonniot, Mallarmé's son-in-law; bought from him by the

Louvre in 1928 for 400,000 francs, 100,000 of which were given by the Society of Friends of the Louvre.

Manet and Mallarmé had known each other since 1874, in which year the latter published an article in the *Renaissance* entitled 'The hanging committee for the 1874 Salon and Monsieur Manet' in which he defended the painter. Manet's reply was brief: 'Thank you. If only I had several defenders like you the judges could go and . . . themselves!' As a gesture of gratitude, he illustrated in 1875 Mallarmé's translation of Edgar Allan Poe's *The Raven*. This was the start of a firm friendship between poet and painter. In 1876 Manet illustrated *L'Après-midi d'un Faune*. This collaboration was termed by one critic 'criminal complicity.'

Manet and Mallarmé lived near one another. Every day, on his way home from teaching, Mallarmé would spend the rest of the afternoon with the painter, and topics of conversation never flagged between these two sensitive intellects, who understood and complemented each other so well. Manet's death was a great grief to the poet. In 1884 he wrote to Verlaine: 'I have for the last twenty years seen my dear friend Manet every day. I can't believe he is no longer here.'

Renoir also painted Mallarmé. It is not a good likeness (Louvre, on loan to the Versailles Museum).

Mallarmé in this portrait is smoking a cigar, one of his favourite pleasures. I cannot refrain from quoting the poet's own words:

'I see the story of our souls in the light, slow exhalations of a cigar, in ring after ring of smoke, vanishing the one into the next. The cigar will burn gaily on, provided you take care that the ash does not get separated from the bright kiss of the fire.'

The Blonde with Bare Breasts. Signed and painted in 1876–1878
Canvas: 24¹/₂ × 20 in. (62 × 51 cm.) Cat. R.F. 2637

This picture was sold by Madame Manet to Ambroise Vollard on March 26, 1894, for 500 francs; he sold it to Moreau-Nélaton who in 1927 gave it to the Louvre where it was entered in 1934, after having been shown temporarily at the Museum of Decorative Arts with the pictures acquired in 1906.

Portrait of Clemenceau   *Serveuse de Blocks*

We do not know the date of this voluptuous portrait. Some art historians (Jamot, Moreau-Nélaton) place it in 1875, others, including Tabarant, in 1878. The identity of the lady is also uncertain. Those who date it 1875 presumed that Ellen Andrée (the actress who posed for Degas' *Absinthe,* see page 139) was the model. But the two faces are too different for this to be a tenable hypothesis. Tabarant declares that the young woman is called Marguerite. On the other hand, Madame Manet's account book gives the following indication: 'Vollard, 1894, March 26. Not paid. Amélie-Jeanne, nude bust (sic), for 500 francs.' According to Edmond Bazire, Amélie-Jeanne was a professional model who posed for painters round about 1876–80.

In any case, this picture belongs to Manet's later work. His manner began to change after 1872. He gave up his fine, sombre works to follow the *peinture claire* of the Impressionists. He even went so far as to paint out-of-doors though he had previously jeered at Monet for painting people against a natural background. But nature never succeeded in distracting Manet from his favourite subject, human beings. It is, however, rare for him to return to the nude, and since his youth, the period of the *Picnic* (see page 114) and *Olympia* (see page 116) where the pose and the nudity were inspired by the *Venus of Urbino* at the Uffizi, he had abandoned the nude in its entirety. The nudity of this beautiful blonde, more dreamy than sad, is far from being an academic nude, a nude of the schools. She is rather someone who has just undressed, as shown by the chemise which

has fallen from her shoulders, and also by the little straw hat ornamented with poppies which she has not had time to take off. She also posed for the few other nudes of this period; the *Tub,* where she is seen from the back and down to the waist, and the *Garter* where she only reveals an ample *décolleté.*

126

Portrait of Cabaner   *Crystal Vase with Flowers*   *Portrait of Madame Emile Zola*

On the Beach. Signed and dated 1873
Canvas: 23 ¹/₂ × 28 ¹/₂ in. (60 × 72 cm.) Cat. R.F. 1953–24

Sold by Manet to Henri Rouart on November 8, 1873 (1500 Fr.); Henri Rouart sale, December 9–11, 1912, No. 237 (92,000 Fr.); sold to M. A. Fajard; Jacques Doucet collection; Madame Jacques Doucet collection; Dubrujeaud collection; given to the Louvre by Monsieur Dubrujeaud in 1953; entered the museum in 1970.

The sun-worship which drives hordes of holiday-makers to the Mediterranean coast in the hottest months of the year did not manifest itself till after the first world war; previously, one had only visited the Côte d'Azur in the winter. On the other hand, the northern beaches, particularly along the Channel coast, were regarded as especially salubrious on account of the high iodine content of the air, and were popular holiday places during the summer. Manet used to go to Boulogne-sur-mer with his family in mid-July, and there he painted seascapes and still-life studies of fish.

In 1873, however, he rented a villa for three weeks at Berk-Plage, another Channel resort; and, enjoying the opportunity to relax, he painted several marine studies during his stay. These are some of his finest landscapes. This period did in fact provide a respite in his bitter struggle against the selection committee and the public; *Le Bon Bock,* exhibited at the Salon in the same year, was well received. His wife and his brother posed for the two lightly-indicated figures, whose only function is to create two successive planes in order to establish the sea in the background. Few pictures better express this genius for synthesis which enabled Manet in his early period to distil the essence from the many aspects of a given scene, and thus concentrate reality into a picture – a quality also found in the Japanese prints which inspired him.

Butterfly Hunt

The Cornfield

The Cradle. Painted in 1873
Canvas: 21¹/₂ × 18 in. (55 × 46 cm.) Cat. R.F. 2849

It was in the Salon of 1874; then belonged to Madame Pontillon, born Edma Morisot, then to her daughter, Madame Forget; it was bought from her by the Louvre in 1930 for 300,000 francs.

Berthe Morisot was born into a well-to-do bourgeois family. Her father was an official. With great gifts for painting she received every encouragement from her mother. She copied pictures in the Louvre, then two years later, wanting to work direct from nature, she received some advice from Corot who became as a result an intimate friend of the Morisots at their house in Passy.

In 1868 she met Manet, who was introduced to her by Fantin-Latour. Following his example she became more eager to paint faces and portraits. Manet lured her into the Impressionist movement but she was never his pupil. They influenced one another, and it was partly due to Berthe Morisot that Manet abandoned his sombre manner and brightened his palette.

In 1874 she married Eugène Manet, the painter's brother, but continued to paint, for in the same year she agreed, despite her success in the official Salons, to take part in the first exhibition of the Impressionist

group, which was held at the house of Nadar, the photographer. She remained faithful to the group and took part in almost all their exhibitions.

In 1874 she sent in this *Cradle*. It was inspired by a pose of her sister, Edma, Madame Pontillon, who like herself had begun a career as a painter and had had the same masters as Berthe. But her marriage in 1869 to a naval officer stationed at Lorient, prevented her continuing. Berthe was very fond of her sister and painted her several times. The Louvre possesses a portrait of Edma done in pastel and a *Butterfly Hunt* (page 129) which shows the young woman playing with her children in an orchard.

Berthe Morisot brought to the Impressionist group a touch of sentiment which goes back to the oldest traditions of French art.

EVA GONZALÈS, 1849–1883

A Box at the Théâtre des Italiens   *The Pink Negligee*

EDGAR DEGAS, 1834–1917

Portrait of a young Woman. Signed and painted in 1867
Canvas: 10$^{1}/_{2} \times$ 8$^{1}/_{2}$ in. (27 $\times$ 22 cm.) Cat. R.F. 2430

Shown at the third of the Impressionist exhibitions in 1877 (No. 53); in the collection of Georges Viau, Paris; Wilhelm Hansen, Copenhagen; Herman Heilbuth, Copenhagen; acquired by the Louvre in 1924, for 100,000 francs; in the Luxembourg, and the Louvre in 1929.

The date of this portrait has not been decided. Some art historians place it about 1868–70, others about 1860–62. Some even think Degas painted it at the age of twenty-five in 1859 or else about 1872. Judging by the hair-style, one would place it in about 1866–67.

Uncertainty about the date is paralleled by uncertainty about the sitter. Paul Jamot considered she greatly resembled Baroness Bellelli, born Laura Degas, the artist's aunt. Monsieur Guérin thinks he recognises another sister of Degas' father, Rose-Aurore, but she would have been about sixty.

Both historians and critics unite, however, in praising the interest and

131

beauty of the portrait. Georges Rivière, in the review *Impressionnisme* (1877), noted already that: 'At the exhibition Monsieur Degas has a portrait of a woman painted some years ago. This portrait is a marvel of drawing, It is as beautiful as the most beautiful of Clouets, the greatest of the primitives.' François Clouet or Corneille de Lyon are often used thus by the great Degas specialist, Monsieur P. A. Lemoisne, for comparison. Paul Jamot compares it to a portrait by Holbein, because of the firm precision and the exactitude of the drawing. 'But this draughtsman is also a pain-

ter ... to-day this Holbein makes us think of Vermeer, but a less placid Vermeer, more interested in the deeper meanings of life.'
Among all these comparisons, the best seems to be the one referring to Clouet; it shows how the traditional virtues of the French school came to life again with Degas, who closely studied the old masters.

The Bellelli Family. Painted about 1858–1859
Canvas: 78³/₄ × 98³/₈ in. (200 × 250 cm.) Cat. R.F. 2210

This picture never left Degas' studio, where it was found after his death; it was bought by the Nation for 300,000 francs before the first

sale of the contents of Degas' studio (6th to 8th May 1918), 50,000 francs of this was contributed by the Count and Countess de Fels; Monsieur René de Gas had lowered the original reserve price in order to keep the picture in France; it became part of the Luxembourg collection in 1918 and was transferred to the Louvre in 1929.

It was in Florence that the idea came to Degas to paint the Bellelli family. Degas' aunt, his father's sister, born Laura Degas, had married the Baron de Bellelli, and Degas was staying in her house. He had already in 1856 and again in 1857, at either Naples or Florence, made sketches, drawings, studies which he would make use of later on for his big family portrait. This idea began to take shape in 1858–59. A visit to Florence, which was to have lasted a few days, lengthened into weeks, then into months. He first of all intended to make a portrait of his aunt, but in the end he collected and grouped together on a single immense canvas all the separate portraits.

The work certainly dates from after the death (August 31, 1858) of René-Hilaire Degas, father of the Baroness de Bellelli, who is shown in mourning like her two daughters. According to Ricardo Raimondo the canvas, which had been delivered to the family at Naples, suffered damage; Degas took it rolled up to Paris for repairs and forgot about it. It was only discovered in 1918 during the sale of the contents of his studio.

In this work, which he painted at the age of twenty-five, Degas used for the first time those boldly unorthodox methods of composition by means of which he tried to express the unexpected element in life.

The Duchesse Morbilli   *Hilaire-René de Gas*   *Mademoiselle Dihau at the P*

The Dancing Class   *The Lady with a Flower Vase*

The Musicians in the Orchestra. Signed and painted about 1868–1869
Canvas: 22 × 18 in. (56.5 × 46 cm.) Cat. R.F. 2417

Painted for Degas' friend Dihau; in Mademoiselle Dihau's collection;
acquired from her in 1923. She kept it, as well as her own portrait by Degas,
during her lifetime for a rent of 12,000 francs; in the Louvre in 1935.

Wishing to follow in the footsteps of Ingres, whom he greatly admired,
Degas wanted to devote himself to the arts of portraiture and the painting
of historical scenes. The Louvre possesses two of the five historical compositions which he painted, *Semiramis building a Town,* and the *Misfortunes
of the Town of Orleans,* both very early works. After 1865, however, he
abandoned this kind of painting to which he was not suited and, until the
Franco-Prussian war in 1870, painted mainly portraits. Degas only painted
members of his family or close friends. Among the latter he painted musicians especially. His very artistic father gave small musical parties every
Monday. Thus it was that he did the portrait of *Mademoiselle Dihau at the
Piano* (see page 134), the singer Pagans, the cellist Pillet (see page 140) and
so on. Then he thought of painting a group in the orchestra pit at the
Opera, an ensemble of his friends in the setting of their work. It was a
bold and hitherto unexploited notion to draw attention to that part of the
theatre which is usually poorly lighted and sacrificed to the stage. From this
idea springs his *Musicians in the Orchestra*. In front can be seen his friend

Dihau, a bassoonist and brother of Marie Dihau, the pianist. Gouffé, the double-bass, is seen from the back; on the left is Pillet, the cellist; next to Dihau, Altès the flautist, then the first violins and also some friends of Degas, a painter, a doctor, a student, whom Degas introduced into the orchestra to complete his gallery of portraits. The box on the left is occupied by Chabrier, the composer. It was while painting this scene that Degas, with his painter's eye, crossed the footlights for the first time and discovered the artificial lighting and the dancers performing their steps above the heads of the musicians in the orchestra.

The Foyer de la Danse at the Rue Le Peletier Opera.
Signed and painted in 1872
Canvas: 12 1/2 × 18 in. (32 × 46 cm.) Cat. R.F. 1977

   This picture was in the collections of Durand-Ruel; Manzi; A. Veyer;
and was acquired by the Count de Camondo in 1894; given by him to
the Louvre in 1908; put into the collection in 1911; and shown in 1914.
   In 1868 Degas made his first contact with the stage of the Opera
(*Musicians in the Orchestra,* page 136). Next he went behind the scenes.

But before painting a dancer performing, he studied her at work in the practice room. This *Foyer de la Danse* is the first of his pictures of dancers and like the *Orchestra*, also the earliest of its kind, one of the most perfect. Far from noise and from the public, in this room with bare walls decorated with a frieze and pilaster in marble, the young ballerinas are working or resting. The ballet master, in white working clothes, directs the steps of a dancer, emphasising his orders with a big stick, while a violinist prepares to accompany the dance which is about to begin.

This small picture is a masterpiece of harmony and discretion, reminding one in its finesse of Vermeer. It is apparently composed in the classic tradition, for the touch is sharp, the outlines very clean and definite. But it is, in fact, in the composition that one finds the painter has taken liberties, first of all in the matter of the large empty space in the middle which cuts the scene in two and divides attention between the exercising dancers on the left and the group round the professor on the right. He is surrounded by dancers, one collapsed on a chair, the rest either attentive or indifferent to the lesson. Besides this large empty space, which shocked people at that date, there was also an empty chair in the middle of the composition, which shocked them even more.

The public of that time did not understand that this great deserted space is needed for the spectator to be able to follow in imagination the steps of the dancers. The open door on the left reveals a glimpse of a tulle skirt and is a detail which adds still more life and movement to the picture.

Absinthe. Signed and painted in 1876
Canvas: $36^1/_4 \times 26^3/_4$ in. (92 $\times$ 68 cm.) Cat. R.F. 1984

This is perhaps the picture which appeared in the second Impressionist exhibition, entitled *In a Café,* and which once belonged to Mr. Arthur Kay of Glasgow (a letter from Mr. Kay informs us that Degas called his picture *At the Café*); it passed into the collection of Count Isaac de Camondo in whose notebook we find the following information: '*The Apéritif* by Degas (Martin), May 1893, 21,000 francs.' It was bequeathed by Camondo to the Louvre in 1908, entered in 1911 and exhibited in 1914.

From 1876 onwards, the Impressionist painters to some extent deserted

the Café Guerbois and met at the New Athens in the Place Pigalle near the Cirque Fernando. Monet and Sisley were the only painters of the group who never went there. Manet and Degas enjoyed going there. Pissarro, Cézanne, and the musician Cabaner appeared occasionally. Marcellin Desboutin, the engraver, also used to go there. This, then, is the setting chosen by Degas for *Absinthe*. The two figures in the picture are not anonymous drinkers, but friends of Manet and Degas, and had agreed to pose for Degas. They were Desboutin and Ellen Andrée, the latter a well-known actress in her day who did not flinch from this new role which required her to become ugly with a stupid tired expression and to wear clumsy boots and a frayed coat and skirt. Beside her appears the outline of a man, his features brutalised by alcohol.

The presence in Paris of the engraver, back from Florence, and the shape of the actress's hat, help to establish the date for this picture as 1876. It recalls irresistibly the atmosphere of Zola's *L'Assommoir* which was published in 1877.

Here again the set-up is out of alignment. The figures do not face the viewer but are placed along a rising oblique line. They are separated from the spectator by a rampart of café tables in white marble filling the entire foreground and cutting across one another at right angles. A few objects have been placed on them, two rolled-up newspapers, a matchbox, a carafe and a glass of absinthe.

In 1893 the British owner of this picture sent it to an exhibition in London. Its realism was considered vulgar and it provoked such a scandal that its owner hastened to get rid of it.

Marguerite de Gas	*Portrait of Valernes*	*The Cellist Pillet*

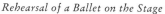
Rehearsal of a Ballet on the Stage   *The Chorus*

At the Races, in front of the Stands. Signed and painted about 1869–1872
Canvas: 18 × 24 in. (46 × 61 cm.) Cat. R.F. 1981

In the Faure and Durand-Ruel collections; acquired by Camondo in 1894; bequeathed to the Louvre in 1908 and added to the collection in 1914.

It was when staying with his friends the Valpinçons in 1860 at their château of Ménil-Hubert in Normandy near the Du Pin training stables in a countryside of horse breeding and race meetings, that Degas discovered the horse in action and made countless sketches of horsemen and horse-women, hunt meets and jockeys preparing to race. In 1862 he painted the *Gentlemen's Race* now in the Louvre.

This picture shows one of Degas' numerous experiments in technique. Here he has painted with *essence* (probably turpentine) on canvas. The result is an increased brightness and clearness in the whole range of colours.

The date of this picture is disputed. Some authorities give it as 1869–72, but Paul-André Lemoisne puts it at 1879 in his catalogue. It may be the same picture as the one called *Racehorses* (No. 63) at the fourth Impressionist exhibition. The way the scene is presented fits this date well.

The horse is a favourite subject in the nineteenth century. Gros and Delacroix had both expressed their idea of the horse in heroic terms. Géricault saw in the horse a symbol of power. For Carle Vernet and Alfred de Dreux it is a pretext for painting the elegance of fashion. But all these artists kept to the immemorial traditions and conventions, such as the 'flying gallop'. Degas was the first, thanks to photography, who was able to

141

examine minutely the different movements of the animal and thus observe correctly its various attitudes. What interested him in horses and dancers alike was the theme of *instability*, which also haunted Monet when he painted the variations of light in the constantly changing sky. Towards the end of his life Degas did a number of horse statuettes in bronze.

The Louvre also possesses two racing studies from the Camondo collection both of which are very early.

At the Races
(Amateur Jockeys)

Women ironing. Signed and painted about 1884
Canvas: 30 × 31⁷/₈ in. (76 × 81 cm.) Cat. R.F. 1985

This picture was in the Gallimard, Manzi, and Camondo collections (from Camondo's notebook: 'The *Laundresses* by Degas from the Gallimard and Manzi collections. November 1893. 25,000 francs.'); bequeathed by Camondo to the Louvre in 1908 and put in the collection in 1911; exhibited in 1914.

If, despite the fact that he never painted out-of-doors, Degas can be ranked among the Impressionists, it is because of his taste for modern subjects, his passion for analysis, and his endeavour to capture the fleeting moment. Horse races and the gyrations of dancers are the answers to these desires, but there are other subjects which suit his acute powers of observation, such as the professional habits of pedicures, modistes, laundresses, whose movements he never tired of studying.

In 1869 he painted a *Woman Ironing* for the first time (Louvre, Personnaz collection). After that date he continued to exploit this theme which he succeeded in varying to the most astounding extent by changing the pose, the setting, and above all the lighting — the play of light, which he diversified as much as possible by means of artificial illumination — transparencies and reflections from the washing.

The *Laundresses* in the Louvre gives the lie to the Goncourts' poetic evocation: 'The rose of the flesh in the white of the linen.' For in fact the first washerwoman, a great, strapping wench, is yawning and stretching, with one hand holding her head, and with a bottle of wine in the other. In front of her there is neither washing nor iron. She is obviously exhausted

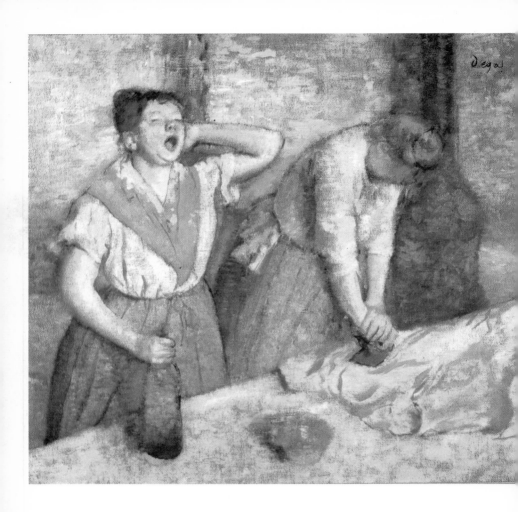

and overwhelmed by the heat. Her companion wearily continues at her task. The Goncourts wrote of this picture: 'Degas puts laundresses before us and explains to us in technical terms the application of the hot iron, from above, from below, etc.'

Degas' treatment of this theme recalls the realism that was the vogue in literature just then. *Manette Salomon* of the Goncourts (1867) and above all *L'Assommoir* (1877) in which Zola describes in detail the laundry belonging to Gervaise, where 'big Clemence was ironing her thirty-fifth man's shirt.'

Madame Jeantaud at a Mirror. Signed and painted about 1875
Canvas: 27³/₄ × 31⁵/₈ in. (70 × 80 cm.) Cat. R.F. 1970–38

Madame Jeantaud collection; Doucet collection; Madame Doucet collec-
tion; Dubrujeaud collection. Bequeathed to the Louvre in 1968 by Monsieur
Dubrujeaud, with usufruct reserved for his nephew Monsieur Angladon-
Dubrujeaud, who handed it over to the Louvre in 1970.

The young woman has just dressed to go out, and is giving a final glance in her mirror to make sure that all is in order. This gives Degas a pretext for painting a portrait both full-face and in lost profile.

The fugitive outline of the actual figure is hardly more substantial than its reflection; the picture is not so much a portrait as a piece of artistic research. A little later, in about 1877, Degas painted a more exact likeness of Madame Jeantaud in which she is represented full face.

The history of Degas' painting is to a large extent the history of his friendships. He was given to sarcasm, and was not of a very sociable disposition, but he remained faithful to a small circle of friends, and used to choose his models from among them. They were not pictures he sold.

Degas had formed a friendship with the engineer Jeantaud in Henri Rouart's battery, in which he had served as a gunner during the siege of 1870. It was at Jeantaud's house that he met Madame Jeantaud's cousin, the Vicomte Lepic, the subject of one of his most daring portraits. He also painted Jeantaud with two of his comrades in the battery, Liné and Lainé; this picture was presented to the Louvre in 1929 by Madame Jeantaud.

The wife's portrait came to join that of her husband in the Jeu de Paume in circumstances which I find very moving. In 1959 Monsieur Dubrujeaud, who had inherited from Madame Doucet *Madame Jeantaud at a Mirror* and Manet's *On the Beach,* offered to donate one of these paintings to the Louvre, with usufruct, and left the choice of picture to me. My personal preference was for *Madame Jeantaud,* but I resolved to choose *On the Beach.* Monsieur Dubrujeaud, however, included the portrait in his bequest.

The Tub

After the Bath

MARY CASSATT, 1845–1926

Young Woman Sewing

Mary Cassatt, an American of French upbringing, was initially influenced by Degas, particularly by the composition of his pictures; but her optimistic temperament subsequently inclined her towards Renoir, as one can clearly see in this painting (dating from about 1886). Her favourite theme is motherhood, which she depicts without any sentimentality, seeing it as an expression of life and health.

CLAUDE MONET, 1840–1926

Le Déjeuner sur l'herbe (fragment) *(The Picnic).* Painted in 1865
Canvas: 164½ × 59 in. (418 × 150 cm.) Cat. R.F. 1957–7

In the Michel Monet and Georges Wildenstein collections; given by Monsieur Wildenstein to the Louvre in 1957.

In 1865, no doubt to challenge Manet who had shown a *Picnic* (page 114) at the Salon in 1863, Monet dreamed of showing also at the Salon a gigantic work showing people picnicking in the forest of Fontainebleau.

In April he settled at Chailly-en-Bière on the edge of the forest and started a colossal undertaking which he worked at in the village inn from preliminary sketches, of which one picture in the Moscow Museum appears to have been the largest. (It measures 1.30 m. × 1.81 m., 51" × 71"). By the end of the summer the undertaking had progressed considerably. Courbet, an expert on large compositions, was generous with advice to the artist.

A different picture, *Camille,* was sent to the 1866 Salon. More than fifty years later, in 1920, Monet showed the Duke of Treviso the central portion of a picture of 1865 in his studio at Giverny and related how, being unable to pay his board, he had left the canvas with the landlord,

who had rolled it up and put it in the cellar, where he (Monet) found it ruined by damp. He cut out the central group and discarded the rest.

This central fragment (2.48 m.×2.17 m., 98″×85½″) had long been the only part known. But some years ago another fragment, the left part, was found in the studio at Giverny by Monsieur Georges Wildenstein who has given it to the Louvre. It enables one, better perhaps than the central fragment preserved in a Paris collection, to reconstruct the atmosphere of the whole work. This special quality of light filtered by foliage is the real subject of the picture. As far as one can judge, Monet's *Picnic* was to have measured about 4.60 m.×6 m. (180″×228″), or more than 30 square yards.

The Cart. Road under Snow at Honfleur. Signed and painted about 1865
Canvas: 25 1/2 × 36 1/4 in. (65 × 92 cm.) Cat. r.f. 2011

Bought by Count Isaac de Camondo, at the Abbé Gauguin's sale on May 6, 1901, for 7,260 francs (according to the Count's notebooks);

bequeathed by him to the Louvre in 1908; accepted in 1911; on view in 1914.

Just as Courbet 'discovered' Boudin by noticing in a shop front in Le Havre some small landscapes by him, so Boudin himself noticed at a framer's in Le Havre some amusing caricatures. Their author, Monet, then a youth of fifteen, was not aware of his true vocation. Boudin took him to paint out-of-doors near Honfleur. 'It was like the rending of the veil,' said Monet later, 'I realised what painting could be.' Boudin was not the only one to open his eyes. Monet was greatly impressed by the watercolours of Jongkind.

Some of the Romantic painters (Isabey, Huet, Delacroix) had followed the example of British artists and had come to paint the estuary of the Seine. Isabey, in his turn, brought Jongkind. To Honfleur, besides Boudin and Monet, came Courbet, Sisley and Bazille. They all stayed at 'Mother' Toutain's, at the Saint-Siméon farm. It was there that different influences, especially that of the sea, formed Claude Monet as a painter.

This road, seen in perspective is, in fact, the one leading to the Saint-Siméon farm, which almost deserves to give its name to a school of painting.

In painting snow pictures, Monet was following the example of Courbet, but his snow is more natural than that of the painter of deer. Monet painted the same snowbound road at least three times, probably during the same winter. None of these pictures is dated. In 1867, we know for certain he was at Honfleur during the winter. However a letter written by him in the Louvre, indicates that he painted it in 1865. Beside the cart, Monet placed a small figure which he afterwards covered up, but which has emerged a little from beneath the snow. It is very distinct under X-rays,

Still-life   *Farmyard in Normandy*

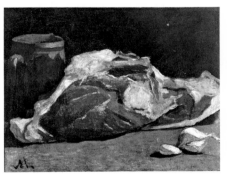 

Women in the Garden. Signed and painted in 1866–1867
Canvas: 100¹/₂ × 80³/₄ in. (255 × 205 cm.) Cat. R.F. 2773

Refused by the Salon in 1867; bought from Monet before it was finished
by Frédéric Bazille for 2,500 francs payable in monthly instalments of
50 francs each; it remained in Bazille's family at Montpellier after his
death; exchanged in 1876 for the portrait of Bazille by Renoir (Louvre) in
Monet's possession; given back shortly afterwards to Monet by Manet;
acquired from Monet by the Nation for the Luxembourg in 1921 for the

sum of 200,000 francs; in the Louvre in 1929.

Going beyond what he had done the previous year with the *Picnic* which was too large to be painted out-of-doors, the *Women in the Garden,* smaller but still of exceptional size, was the painter's successful attempt to paint portraits in the open air.

At Ville d'Avray, where he passed the summer of 1866, he had a trench dug in the garden, into which he lowered a huge canvas by means of a pulley, which he manipulated when he wished to paint the top part of his picture, a proceeding regarded with disapproval by Courbet.

Monsieur Gaston Poulain considers the composition to have been inspired by photographs shown to Monet from the family album by Bazille, showing his sister-in-law and three cousins in the garden at Méric. The setting resembles the Bazille family property in Languedoc and the attitude of the young ladies is reminiscent of the poses of the des Hours ladies. Monet's model for all four figures was, however, Camille.

In the autumn of 1866, probably to escape his creditors and to be housed and fed by his parents, Monet left Paris, alone, for Le Havre. He left behind, as he relates, two hundred canvases which he took care to mutilate to prevent them being seized and sold. A letter dated February 2, 1867, written from Honfleur to Boudin by his friend A. Dubourg shows that Monet had taken this picture with him to finish in the studio.

Eventually Bazille's father exchanged it for Renoir's portrait of his son. When Manet returned it to Monet, it was because of a quarrel.

Regatta at Argenteuil. Signed and painted about 1872
Canvas: 19 × 28³/₄ in. (48 × 73 cm.) Cat. R.F. 2778

Bought by Caillebotte for his collection and bequeathed by him to the Louvre in 1894; in the Luxembourg in 1896 and the Louvre in 1929.

With the Franco-Prussian war over, the artists who had scattered met again in Paris in 1871. They settled in the suburbs, joining up with their own particular friends. Pissarro set up house at Pontoise, Monet preferred Argenteuil, to which he was lured by his friend Caillebotte who owned a house there and some boats at Petit-Gennevilliers. Monet lived there from 1872 to 1876, and it was there that he did his most ethereal, fresh and free work. The Seine, with the perpetual movement of the small sailing boats on it, provided the moving light which attracted him as a subject. It was at Argenteuil that the Impressionist technique was really invented. The light is reflected in the rippling water, casts up reflections beneath the arches of the bridges, while the white sails reflected in the river provide a natural example of the separation of strokes and colours. The white streaks of the sails, the red of the roofs, the green of the trees, all dancing in the water make this picture a typical example. Several changes of mind have lightly pushed their way up beneath the paint which covers them.

Renoir often came from either Louveciennes or Paris to join his friend, and both amused themselves by painting the same subjects. Manet also came to Argenteuil from neighbouring Gennevilliers, for he only had to cross the

river, and was initiated in the *peinture claire* technique in 1874. Preferring the human shape to pure landscape, he painted the boatmen. It was there that he depicted Monet painting in his floating studio, built on the principle of Daubigny's *Botin* (Munich Museum).

The name Argenteuil conjures up a whole period, which may be called that of 'pure Impressionism.' These are the last years of research in common. Renoir and Monet both painted at that time a house with a duck pond, and so alike were the two pictures that later they had some trouble in distinguishing their own work! After Argenteuil, the artists drifted apart.

The Louvre has six other pictures painted by Monet at Argenteuil.

The Gare Saint-Lazare. Signed and dated 1877
Canvas: $29^{1}/_{2} \times 39^{1}/_{2}$ in. (75 × 100 cm.) Cat. R.F. 2775

This picture may have been shown at the third Impressionist exhibition in 1877; Gustave Caillebotte acquired it, probably in 1877; he bequeathed it to the Louvre in 1894, and it was entered in the Luxembourg in 1896 and the Louvre in 1929.

On a spring morning during the recent war I was waiting in the deserted station at Le Mans for a train which never came. As I passed the time by watching the movements of a solitary locomotive whose puffs of smoke were coloured pink by the dawn, I felt I was living in a picture by Monet.

The railway, then a great novelty, was often taken as a subject by the Impressionists (Monet, and less often Pissarro and Sisley). It must not be forgotten that these artists who did their work out-of-doors, almost always in the suburbs of Paris, often travelled to their destination by train. They studied with immense interest the play of steam and smoke ceaselessly changing with the wind and the light. For them, in their desire to try and fix the passing moment, the smoke of locomotives, like clouds and reflections in water, was part of that ephemeral universe they had discovered.

There had been forerunners, Turner, in 1844, painted the celebrated *Rain, Steam and Speed* in which a train on a viaduct disappears into the fog. Monet and Pissarro had the opportunity to see this picture in 1870. Turner's train, however, is that of a visionary. Monet's railway scenes are completely real, as their titles indicate: *Railway Bridge at Argenteuil,*

Pont de l'Europe, Arrival of the train from Normandy, Gare Saint-Lazare, etc. The Louvre has another picture of a train in a landscape.

The *Gare Saint-Lazare* especially attracted Monet after 1876.

He showed a series of these views as the third Impressionist exhibition of 1877. He painted seven variations on this theme, and this was the first of his 'series'.

The *Gare Saint-Lazare*, which is in the Louvre thanks to the generosity of Gustave Caillebotte, is the finest of the series. The scintillating luminosity of this picture is obtained by tone division which, so to speak, becomes volatile in coloured spangles.

155

The Bas-Bréau Road

This picture was painted in the forest of Fontainebleau, and is still in the spirit of the Barbizon school. The setting recalls that of *Le Déjeuner sur l'Herbe,* which he was to paint the following year at Chailly-en-Bière.

A Field of Poppies

A Corner of an Apartment

The Argenteuil Basin

Turkeys   *Chrysanthemums*

Snow Effect at Vétheuil. Signed and painted about 1878–1879
Canvas: 20¹/₂ × 27¹/₂ in. (52 × 70 cm.) Cat. R.F. 3755

This picture was no doubt shown at the fourth Impressionist exhibition in 1879 where No. 144 had this name and a notice 'to H. C.'; it was in the Caillebotte collection; given by Caillebotte to the Louvre in 1894; transferred to the Luxembourg in 1896 and shown at the Louvre in 1933.

In 1878 Claude Monet left Argenteuil, where he had lived for six years, to settle in Vétheuil which, being farther from Paris, gave him more isolation and a more rural atmosphere. He stayed till 1882 and painted many views of the village, from the opposite bank of the river, and at all times of the year. The very severe winter of 1880 gave him the opportunity to paint landscapes of snow and ice. The Seine bearing ice floes on its current inspired the *Débacles,* which he continued in other surroundings.

His stay at Vétheuil was a time of transition for his art. The Argenteuil period, was Impressionist, instinctive, lyrical, while the period of Giverny after Vétheuil found him interpreting nature in a reflective, deliberate way.

It is above all in these winter landscapes that the evolution of Monet's technique can be admired. His first snow scenes recall Courbet (see the *Cart,* page 149). The artist's vision is more in line with tradition. The colour is spread over large surfaces. But in the *Débacles,* which links with this winter view of Vétheuil, the brush-strokes are broken up and make a vibrating whole, with the pieces of ice mixing in with the grey water. Later his manner changed again. Fluidity and separation of tones gave place to a more precise impasto.

Twenty years later, living at Giverny, Monet sometimes returned to the

subjects which had inspired him. Thus, there is in the Louvre a view of Vétheuil painted in 1901 and taken from the same viewpoint. It is a summer sunset this time, just an excuse for depicting a play of light. The contours are vague, and the outline of the village is barely discernible (see page 161).

Rouen Cathedral. Bright Sunshine. Signed and dated 1894
Canvas: 42 × 28³/₄ in. (107 × 73 cm.) Cat. R.F. 2002

In December 1894 Count de Camondo was brought by Manzi to Monet's studio and bought four of his Rouen cathedral pictures; according to the entries in his notebooks he paid 50,000 francs for the four; he left them to the Louvre in 1908, and they were shown there in 1914; in 1907 the Nation bought one of Monet's cathedrals; the Louvre therefore owns five out

of the twenty that Monet painted.

Light was all that interested Monet. In order to pin down this phenomenon he painted all the variations possible on a single subject. After having, in 1890, observed the haystacks in a field in Giverny in all weathers, then, on the banks of the Epte, painted the poplars at different times of the day, he took for his subject a cathedral under the same conditions. In February 1892 he went to live at Rouen above a shop called 'Au Caprice', 81 Rue du Grand-Pont, where the owner, Monsieur Mauquit, rented him a room. He stayed there many months, and from the ever-open window on the first floor he contemplated the principal façade of the cathedral. He reproduced its various aspects in several pictures.

His technique was still changing; his paint became a sort of stippled cement as if to imitate the grain of the old stones. The picture reproduced here was painted in full sunshine. Others were done in a grey dawn, or at twilight, in the fires of sunset, or again all veiled in mist.

The following year, 1893, Monet returned to Rouen and continued his variations on this theme, then he finished the work at Giverny.

His letters testify to the trouble he took. 'I work as hard as I can but what I have undertaken is enormously difficult.' 'My stay here is drawing near its close. This does not mean that I am ready to finish my cathedrals. Alas, the more I go on the more difficult I find it to put down what I feel. It is forced labour, searching, testing, not achieving very much.' Still anxious to perfect his series, he only finished it two years later, continually postponing the exhibition he had arranged at Durand-Ruel's.

Rocks at Belle-Ile　　　　　　　　　　　　　　　　*The Boat*

Water-lilies. Harmony in Rose   *Vétheuil. Sunset*

CAMILLE PISSARRO, 1830–1903

The Edge of the village. Signed and dated 1872
Canvas: 17³/₄ × 21¹/₂ in. (45 × 55 cm.) Cat. R.F. 2436

Bought by Ernest May from the artist; May sale June 4, 1890 (No. 57); bought back again by May for 2,100 francs according to Tabarant; given by May to the Louvre in 1923 and hung in 1926 as the centre part of a triptych, accompanied by Monet's *Pleasure Boats* and Sisley's *Ile Saint-Denis;* these three pictures are contemporary and of the same size and were thus shown in a unique setting in May's house and this arrangement has been kept.

Pissarro, back from England in 1871, returned to Louveciennes. His joy at being back in France can be inferred from the serenity and calm of his pictures at that time. This *Edge of the Village* (which was thought to be Louveciennes but which is more probably Voisins near by) shows Pissarro's constructive spirit at work, using this motif of the village and arranging it to suit his purpose, which was, like Corot's, to express space in depth Renoir and Sisley even more (pages 170, 173, 174) were also attracted by this traditional theme. Monet cared less for it. He preferred to express space in width rather than depth, and after 1880 was always seeking wide effects.

The Louvre possesses several *Roads,* more or less of the same date (the *Coach* from the Moreau-Nélaton collection, the *Ennery Road* from the Charpentier donation) but none is as gay and lighthearted as this one. Instead of a damp autumn evening which makes the horses flounder about as in the *Coach,* the scene is a fine afternoon at the end of the winter. The sky is free from clouds, the clean light percolates everywhere. The air is dry. The shadows thrown by great tree trunks form a series of parallel streaks which cut across the passage of a manure-cart. Against the sky pread out branches with buds just forming.

The motif is modest and simple, but the firm construction is combined with a softness in the atmosphere of the picture, which announces the coming of spring. The new element in this picture is the treatment of light.

The Louveciennes Road

At Louveciennes, where he lived after the war of 1870, Pissarro painted in a brisk and lively manner a whole series of unpretentious works on a theme inherited from Corot — namely, the road: the winding road, or the road in perspective. It was at this period he discovered that the most brilliant light is that of winter.

The Red Roofs. Signed and dated 1877
Canvas: 21 × 25¼ in. (53 × 64 cm.) Cat. R.F. 2735

In the Caillebotte collection under the name of *A Corner of the Village,* bequeathed by Caillebotte to the Louvre in 1894; exhibited at the Luxembourg in 1896 and at the Louvre in 1929.

After the Franco-Prussian war, Pissarro only remained at Louveciennes for one more year before making up his mind to settle at Pontoise, where he remained for twelve years (1872–84) although he kept on his studio in Montmartre. He shared from then on the Impressionist theories but let Monet, haunted by water and the reflections made in it by the light, settle at Argenteuil, taking Renoir and Sisley with him. He himself was closer in spirit to the earth and the peasants, and more attentive to constructive values in his painting. Cézanne, Guillaumin, and later, Gauguin, were therefore attracted to him. The subject of houses seen through trees was used by Pissarro from 1868 onwards. The clean construction of the houses is broken up by bare branches forming a kind of diaphanous tracery. Through this poetic screen, we see the solid mass of grouped buildings, their roofs bright and gay beneath the winter sun. The dominating hillside of the Hermitage is close at their elbow. Its crest is outlined against a narrow band of blue sky. This winter effect is achieved by a magnificent

163

clarity of design, which is the difference between a picture by Pissarro and one by Monet on the same subject.

Neither human being nor animal draws the eye away from the principal subject. Before 1870 Pissarro had been inclined to work in fluid colours and half-impasto in the manner of Corot. In the Pontoise period, he was more ready to use a mass of stipple worked over with a thicker brush. This technique he owed, doubtless, to the continued influence of Cézanne who left him at the beginning of 1874. In 1954, at an exhibition at the Musée de l'Orangerie devoted to the painters of Auvers-sur-Oise, I placed next to one another pictures done in this manner by Cézanne and Pissarro. They were so much alike that one could easily confuse them.

Kitchen Garden. Trees in Blossom. Signed and dated 1877
Canvas: 25¹/₂ × 32¹/₄ in. (65 × 82 cm.) Cat. R.F. 2733

In the Caillebotte collection; bequeathed by Caillebotte to the Louvre in 1894; exhibited at the Luxembourg in 1896, and at the Louvre in 1929.

It was at Pontoise in 1872 that Pissarro initiated Cézanne into the mysteries of painting in bright colours, a veritable conversion on the part of the painter from Aix-en-Provence, committed as he was to his dark hues. Cézanne, who esteemed Pissarro very highly, said that of all the painters 'he was in the closest touch with nature.' Later, he recalled Pissarro in these moving words: 'He was both humble and very great, in some ways rather like God.'

The two artists, whose influence over each other was henceforth mutual, often painted the same scenes. This picture was painted at Pontoise itself, at the back of the small house on the Quai du Pothuis where Pissarro lived. The orchard is dominated by the slope of the Hermitage, a massive, well-constructed landscape, very suitable to the temperament of the two artists as they sat side by side painting it. (Cézanne's version never got beyond the stage of a sketch.) Pissarro, with characteristic perseverance, wished to perfect this delicate landscape with its flowers, before rain or a violent wind came and destroyed the scene, while Cézanne, before a landscape like this, considered the graceful decoration of the flowers and blossoms as subsidiary to the shape and moulding of the trunks and branches of the trees, which interested him more.

Pissarro, painting a nature rejoicing in spring colours beneath a blue sky, was particularly sensitive to the beauty of these spring-time orchards, which Monet and Sisley also painted, but less lyrically. This subject had been exploited in several pictures before Pissarro by Daubigny, a great admirer of the Normandy apple orchards. Two years later, Van Gogh at Arles achieved some magnificent pink and white fantasies on this theme.

Woman in a Field. Signed and dated 1887
Canvas: 21 × 25 1/2 in. (54 × 65 cm.) Cat. r.f. 37–47

This picture appeared at the Charles Vignier sale on May 14, 1906, No. 55; it was bought by Antonin Personnaz; bequeathed by Personnaz to the Louvre in 1935 and exhibited in 1937.

Pissarro is often called the 'Master of Eragny' because of the many beautiful landscapes which he painted of that corner of the Vexin where he lived for almost twenty years. During this period he changed his technique several times. This curiosity and incessant anxiety brought on, in 1886, a period of crisis.

Not content with a spontaneous use of the technique of divided tones, as practised by all the Impressionists, he followed with passionate interest the work of Seurat, who applied to this technique a scientific method, derived from the researches of Chevreul. Seurat had no more fervent propagandist than Pissarro. At the mercy of a veritable obsession, he kept trying in vain to convert all his Impressionist friends to this new method. He

accordingly painted several pictures in a pointillist style, not worrying as to what effect this obsession might have on his art as a whole. In 1886 the eighth and last Impressionist exhibition was held. Pissarro did not hesitate to show his own pictures next to the pointillist canvases of Seurat and Signac and painted under the aegis of these two innovators. Félix Fénéon wrote in a critique: 'Pissarro has changed his technique, and now brings to neo-Impressionism a mathematical strictness of analysis and the authority of his name. Henceforth he will systematically break up his tones.'

For the next two years, Pissarro divided and subdivided his tones with zest. His method differed from pointillism in the sense that instead of proceeding by 'dots' of different colours, he employed a sort of 'comma'. The Louvre possesses none of the more resolutely 'divisionist' works of Pissarro; the *Woman in a Field* comes nearest to this technique. One is conscious of a feeling of constraint, despite the particularly brilliant effect.

The Wheelbarrow

Girl with a stick

Landscape at Chaponval

The Church of Knocke

ALFRED SISLEY, 1839–1899

The Road to Sèvres. Signed and dated 1873
Canvas: 21¹/₄ × 29 in. (54 × 73 cm.) Cat. R.F. 2079

In the Peytel collection; given by Peytel, who reserved the use of it for his lifetime, in 1914; in the Luxembourg in 1920, and the Louvre in 1929.

Sisley, with Monet and Pissarro, is the chief representative of Impressionism in the true sense. His landscapes, of an extreme delicacy, are composed in the modern idiom which helped to make his canvases so light and limpid.

Born in Paris, of well-to-do parents, he was sent by his father, an English merchant, to Great Britain to perfect his English and to learn business. He preferred to visit the museums and took little interest in commerce.

Back in Paris in 1862, he used to go to Gleyre's studio where he met Monet, Renoir and Bazille. Until 1870 he was an amateur painter; his output was small for, thanks to his father's money, he did not have to earn his living by it. When the Franco-Prussian war ruined his father, he had to work in earnest and decided to become a painter. Married and the father of a family, he tried to turn his talent to good account, but from this time on he knew the bitterest poverty, getting only the most miserable prices for his pictures. Durand-Ruel, Dr. Viau, and Murer, the confectioner, were his

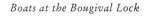

The Ile Saint-Denis   *Boats at the Bougival Lock*

first admirers, and tried to help him but without much success.

From 1871 to 1874 was a rich period for Sisley and his work was of a rare quality. Living near Paris, he was especially the painter of the Ile de France. He painted in turn at Louveciennes, Voisins, Marly, Meudon. He was attracted by the villages bordering the Seine. He knew how to describe the poetic beauty of rivers and their green banks. Tree-bordered roads disappearing into space were a subject which he was always happy to paint, as Corot had already done. *The Road to Sèvres* is one of the best examples. The influence of Corot is noticeable, allied to a new idea of landscape in a clear golden harmony. This simple road with its rows of autumnal trees vanishing into the distance unrolls beneath a sky of a purity and lightness absent from Sisley's landscapes after Monet's influence dulled them round about 1885.

The Flood at Port-Marly. Signed and dated 1876
Canvas: 23⅝ × 32 in. (60 × 81 cm.) Cat. R.F. 2020

This picture belonged to the Poindeson, Pellerin, and Tavernier collections; at the Tavernier sale on March 6, 1900, the picture was bought by Count Isaac de Camondo who bequeathed it to the Louvre in 1908, where it was exhibited in 1914.

The library of the Louvre possesses a copy of the catalogue of the Tavernier sale annotated by Count de Camondo; opposite No. 68, the *Flood*, we read: 'Baught by me, March 6, 1900, for 43,000 francs plus 5 % 2,150 = 45,150 francs.'

The Louvre possesses a large picture, the *Flood at Saint-Cloud*, by Huet, painted twenty years before Sisley's picture. The romantic artist shows the water rising through tall timber in a deserted, desolate countryside.

Claude Monet in his *Débacles* also showed vast solitudes invaded by water and ice.

Sisley, having a more refined sensitivity, places the drama in a region of houses. He painted this subject several times. The large wet surfaces invited those tricks of reflection so dear to the Impressionists. In 1872 he painted three pictures at Port-Marly, including one of the same view as that illustrated. A new flood in 1876 brought him back again and he did five paintings including this one and two others with the same subject: one in the Rouen Museum, the other—also bequeathed by Count de Camondo—in the Louvre. Despite the tragic subject and the black sky presaging further deluges, Sisley, one realises with astonishment, has painted a bright picture.

Poverty haunted Sisley all his life. He could never get more than a few hundred francs for a picture. He died in 1899, unaware that his art would triumph, for only a few months after his death this picture was acquired by Count de Camondo for the enormous sum for those days of 45,150 francs.

Sisley must have realised he would never see this time of triumph for five years previously, when Gustave Geffroy went to see him, he found a dignified, refined and cultivated but also a sad, resigned man, who declared that 'during his lifetime no gleam of glory would ever shine upon his art.'

The Fog

Probably painted at Voisins. It depicts a misty morning in spring, since there are bushes in flower; the mist is silvery and diaphanous, very different from the opaque fog in which Monet was later to shroud the bridges and buildings of London.

Snow at Veneux   *Farmyard* (at Saint-Mammès)

Snow at Louveciennes. Signed and dated 1878
Canvas: 24 × 19¹/₂ in. (61 × 50 cm.) Cat. R.F. 2022

In the Doria and Feydeau collections; at the Feydeau sale on April 4, 1903, Count Isaac de Camondo bought this picture for 11,100 francs; he bequeathed it to the Louvre in 1908; entered in 1911 and exhibited in 1914.

In 1878, Sisley was living at Louveciennes. The following year he left this suburb in close proximity to Paris for Moret-sur-Loing in the Fontainebleau region, where he remained for the next twenty years, until his death. He came under Monet's influence and devoted himself to chromatic researches of a high-flown nature.

This fine snow picture belongs, still, to his light and airy work. The snow is a subject which lends itself well to poetic interpretation. The Impressionists made this subject their own and it was often the principal motive in their researches. It was not Corot who set the example, for he did not care for winter scenes; it was Courbet, who had fallen in love with this season of the year, and painted many aspects of it in his native Jura, buried in winter beneath a thick coating of snow. But Courbet painted frozen landscapes. Claude Monet, one of the leaders of the group, Jongkind, following up the frozen canal pictures of his Dutch ancestors, painted frozen landscape. Claude Monet, one of the leaders of the group, painted several snow scenes at Honfleur in 1865. Then he painted the *Débacles*. Pissarro and Sisley many times depicted perspectives of roads covered with thick or melting snow. In this picture, the snow has just fallen and is still immaculate, with no footprints marring it. It is like cotton wool

173

or felt. Only some tree trunks and the silhouette of a woman walking away mark this unreal décor. The road leads straight into the background.

174

ARMAND GUILLAUMIN, 1841–1927

The Harbour at Charenton   *Paris: Quai de la Gare*

Sunset at Ivry. Signed and painted about 1873
Canvas: 25 ¹/₂ × 32 in. (65 × 81 cm.) Cat. R.F. 1951–34

This picture appeared at the first Impressionist exhibition at Nadar's house in 1874, was in the collection of Dr. Gachet at Auvers-sur-Oise; in the collection of Paul Gachet, and given by him to the Louvre in 1951.

Of rather humble origin, Guillaumin, at twenty, was working for the Paris-Orleans Railway Company. He spent his leisure painting on the banks of the Seine, at Montmartre where he lived, and in the surroundings of Paris. In 1883, he entered the Académie Suisse where he met Cézanne and joined up with Pissarro. The same year he showed work at the Salon des Refusés. He used to go to the Café Guerbois, whose *habitués,* young artists like himself, initiated him into the technique of *peinture claire.* For some time he gave up his job to devote himself to painting but, afraid of the poverty his comrades were fighting, he became a 'Sunday painter'.

He belonged to the independent group which called itself 'Impressionist' and took part in six out of its eight exhibitions. Monet did not think much of his art, but Pissarro defended him faithfully.

In 1892, he was lucky enough to win a big prize in a lottery at the Crédit Foncier. He was able to give up his job to devote himself to painting.

As he grew more mature, his colour passed from blue to bright indigo, and he fell badly into that excess which has been called the 'mania for

violet of the Impressionists.' His chromatism, not without influence on Gauguin, brings him nearer to Fauvism than Impressionism.

But this picture, from the Louvre, does not reveal this later aspect of his art. Sent to the first Impressionist exhibition at Nadar's house in 1874, it was, like the pictures of his friends, the butt of uncomprehending and sarcastic criticism. Dr. Gachet admired him and bought many pictures.

Like Claude Monet at the same period, Guillaumin studied the effects of sunset and sunrise. He also, perhaps, was the first to use factory chimneys as subjects, later painted by Van Gogh and Maximilien Luce.

GUSTAVE CAILLEBOTTE, 1848–1894

Sailing Boats at Argenteuil

Painted in 1888. It was more than ten years later than his friends Renoir and Monet that Caillebotte followed their example and took to painting regattas. He had originally been a realistic painter, and although he was finally won over by Impressionist subject-matter, he never adopted Impressionist techniques.

AUGUSTE RENOIR, 1841–1919

Le Moulin de la Galette. Signed and dated 1876
Canvas: 51¹/₂ × 69 in. (131 × 175 cm.) Cat. r.f. 2739

This picture was shown at the third Impressionist exhibition in 1877 as No. 186; G. Caillebotte collection; bequeathed by Caillebotte in 1894; in the Luxembourg in 1896 and transferred to the Louvre in 1929.

Poised on the Butte Montmartre, the Moulin de la Galette derived its name from being one of those windmills of which there were then several on the Butte; inside it one could once sit and eat the famous cakes. It was an open-air-café where the locals came and danced on Sundays. Students and artists were among them. Intrigued by the mixed character of this cheerful crowd, Renoir wanted to paint it.

In 1876, with this in mind, he sought and found a lodging nearby at 78 Rue Cortot. It had two living rooms and a kind of stable which he could use as a studio. It looked on to a large abandoned garden, with a lawn covered with flowers, and surrounded by big trees. This scene served as background for other portraits, for he remained here till 1880. He started work as soon as he had moved in. 'Every day,' so Georges Rivière, a faithful friend of Renoir and Cézanne, recounts, 'we carried the canvas from the Rue Cortot to the windmill, for the picture was painted in its

entirety on the spot. Things did not always go smoothly. Most of the people in the picture were posed for by Renoir's ordinary models and friends. They were: Estelle, the sister of Jeanne who is seen in the foreground, is sitting on the garden bench. Lamy, Norbert Goeneutte and myself are sitting at a table on which are glasses of grenadine. There were also Gervex, Cordey, Lestringuez, Lhote and others who appear as dancers. Finally, in the centre of the picture, wearing "Merd'Oye" trousers, is a painter of Spanish origin called Solares y Cardenas dancing with Margot.'

As Renoir himself admitted towards the end of his life, the general tonality of this work has been much modified by time. The disappearance of the lake colours which Renoir foolishly mixed with his whites has given the work a predominantly blue colour which it had not got originally.

Renoir made a rapid preparatory sketch for this picture (in a collection near Copenhagen) and another version (0.78 m. × 1.14 m., 31″ × 45″) which belonged to Chocquet and is now in the John Hay Whitney collection, New York.

The Swing. Signed and dated 1876
Canvas: 23¹/₄ × 29 in. (92 × 73 cm.) Cat. R.F. 2738

In the third Impressionist exhibition 1877 (No. 185); Caillebotte collection; bequeathed by Caillebotte in 1894; in the Luxembourg in 1896, and at the Louvre in 1929.

Renoir was an optimistic painter. Love of life, a healthy moral outlook, and cheerful common sense were the basic elements of his character. All this appears in his canvases. Octave Mirbeau said of him: 'Renoir is perhaps the first great artist who never painted a sad picture.' Young women, children, and flowers form the repertory for his compositions. Freshness and *joie de vivre* emanate from each picture. Even his landscapes share this happiness for, with only a few exceptions, he did not paint winter scenes which were sombre and sad. Renoir even said himself: 'For me a picture must be lovable, cheerful and pretty, yes pretty ... There are enough tiresome things in life already without our taking the trouble to produce more.'

The Swing bears witness to this joy in painting. It depicts a fine summer's day. In a park, some cheerful, leisurely groups of people have met. Two young men are talking to a girl standing up on a swing.

An original effect is produced by sunlight coming through the leaves and producing hundreds of tiny speckles on the girl's dress and on the path. In his portraits painted in the open air eight years earlier *(Lise* or the *Bohemian),* Renoir did not produce any effect of this kind. At that time he was still under the influence of Courbet.

The garden which serves as setting for this scene so full of gracefulness is none other than the garden of the Rue Cortot in Montmartre, and the girl is Jeanne, his favourite model at the time, the same girl who sits in

the foreground of the *Moulin de la Galette*, wearing a lovely Chinese dress in blue and red. The two pictures were shown together at the third Impressionist exhibition of 1877. They had been painted almost at the same time. Renoir used to work on this one in the morning in the garden and in the afternoon on the *Moulin de la Galette*.

Nude in the Sunlight. Signed and painted in 1875 or 1876
Canvas: $31^1/_2 \times 25^1/_4$ in. (80 $\times$ 64 cm.) Cat. R.F. 2740

This picture was shown at the second Impressionist exhibition of 1876
under the title of *Study No. 212;* it was in the Caillebotte collection, and

bequeathed to the Louvre in 1894; shown at the Luxembourg in 1896 and at the Louvre in 1929.

Monet was the first, and in his *Picnic,* on a colossal scale, to try and make a success of the effects of light filtered through the undergrowth on the faces and bright clothes of young people. Renoir, later on, must have remembered this attempt by Monet when he undertook the same studies in numerous pictures, the chief of which is the *Moulin de la Galette.*

The *Nude in the Sunlight* preceded the *Moulin.* It cannot have been painted, as has been asserted, in the garden of the Rue Cortot at the same time as the *Swing* (see page 180) while the artist was at the same time finishing the *Moulin* not far away, because it appeared in the second Impressionist exhibition of 1876.

The young sitter was a professional model used by Gervex. Manet used her for *Nana.* Renoir painted her again a little later sitting in a bath (Moscow Museum). Renoir did not hesitate, as he did later in the *Swing,* to show all the marks of light and shade on the flesh producing a strange streaky effect, quite unusual at that date because, for the academic painters, the nude was above all a problem of modelling. It may also be mentioned that the pose, with the model standing in the middle of some foliage, was also quite unexpected at that date. Renoir treats the nude like a landscape, to which times and seasons give different aspects. This picture, therefore, drew the sneers of the critics at the Impressionist exhibition of 1876. The coats of lake colours which have affected many of Renoir's pictures of this period have certainly modified a little the general harmony of the picture.

Renoir also made a rapid sketch with this picture in mind.

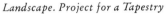

Landscape. Project for a Tapestry   *Banks of the Seine at Champrosay*

Portrait of Madame Alphonse Daudet   *Model*

Woman reading. Signed and painted about 1875–1876
Canvas: 18¹/₂ × 15 in. (47 × 38 cm.) Cat. R.F. 3757

In the Caillebotte collection: bequeathed in 1894, and exhibited in the Luxembourg in 1896 and in the Louvre in 1933.

Renoir was not a revolutionary in the choice of subjects for his pictures nor in his technique. His themes remained those traditional in French art. He often made young women pose in attitudes of reverie, or reading and sewing. These themes, common in France even before the eighteenth century, used over and over again by Corot, derive from the natural tendency of the French school to appreciate the pursuits associated with life indoors. Renoir was particularly inspired by reading till the end of his life. His subjects were the same as those of the academic painters. Chaplin, for instance, painted many women reading.

The model here is unknown, though she appears in several pictures of this period *(Girl with Cat, Woman Sewing, Girl with Lilac)*. It is probably a lamp which throws upon the face of the girl that extraordinary illumination, which is the real subject of the picture.

The spirit in which it is painted reminds one of Fragonard's fantasies in the Louvre. Renoir greatly admired both Fragonard and Boucher. Paul Mantz, speaking of Renoir's work of this period, describes 'those long or broad strokes which make his flesh-tints look like the back of a tapestry.'

The palette is the same as in the *Moulin de la Galette,* which was painted at the same time. In this picture, however, Renoir used a fully or half-charged brush, without glazes. The original colour scheme which allowed a red to predominate has therefore been preserved, and perhaps permits us to realise what the *Moulin de la Galette* was like when it left the artists brush.

Moss Roses. Signed and painted about 1890
Canvas: 13³/₄ × 10¹/₂ in. (35 × 27 cm.) Cat. R.F. 1941–25

In the Viau collection and the Viau sale in 1907; bought by Paul Jamot and bequeathed by him to the Louvre in 1939; exhibited there in 1941.

Flowers played a great part in the development and achievements of

Impressionism. It was unquestionably Renoir who painted them most. Before 1870, he painted mainly wild flowers. In the period which one could label his 'Parisian' or 'worldly' period, he became fascinated by roses. He often decorated his portraits, *Madame Charpentier* or his nudes (see page 190) with them. He was able to nourish his passion for roses after he met Paul Bérard in 1879 in Madame Charpentier's drawing-room, for Bérard was a rose-lover, and grew them on his property of Wargemont in Normandy. Renoir often went to stay with him there in the spring and summer between 1879 and 1885. He painted large compositions of roses for the drawing-room at Wargemont, using the garden roses as models.

Different critics have dated this picture as far apart as 1875 and 1890. The texture, however, forbids such a degree of uncertainty. The technique belongs to the Impressionist period and I personally think that this bouquet was painted about 1880 during the Wargemont period. Later on roses became almost an obsession with Renoir. When Vollard remarked on this with astonishment, Renoir replied: 'I am researching into various flesh tints for my nudes.' He always associated roses with female beauty *(Gabrielle with a Rose)* and with allegorical pictures of spring *(Festival of Pan, Ode to the Flowers)*. He painted them every day during the fine weather at Cagnes, where he grew them on his property, Les Collettes. The Louvre has one of these pictures which may be compared with this one in which the flower is still respected as a model. During the Cagnes period, it is merely an excuse for an exercise in brushwork.

Muslim Festival at Algiers. Signed and dated 1881
Canvas: 28³/₄ × 36⁵/₈ in. (73 × 93 cm.) Cat. R.F. 1957–8

This picture was sold by Renoir to Durand-Ruel in 1892; Claude Monet bought it in 1900; in 1936 Monsieur Georges Wildenstein bought it at Giverny from Monet's family; he sold it in 1955 to Mrs. Margaret Biddle of New York; it was given to the Louvre in June 1957 by the Biddle Foundation, in memory of Margaret Biddle.

In 1880 Renoir, who had hardly left Paris and the district round for some ten years, decided to travel. He visited Italy, then left for Algeria,

attracted by the enthusiastic accounts of his friend Lestringuez. He was the
first of the Impressionists to leave the wet country and changing skies of
the Ile de France and Normandy for the brightness of the Mediterranean
and the East. He wrote to Durand-Ruel (March 1881). 'I want to do some
splendid painting. I shall do before long, I hope. I may be wrong, but if
so I shall be very surprised. I don't want to leave Algiers without bringing
back something of this marvellous country.' He stayed six weeks in Algiers,
and brought back several remarkable pictures. The Louvre possesses

another, acquired in 1943. This picture has become famous under the title of the *Kasbah in Algiers,* which was only given to it when it became the property of Mrs. Biddle.

It was previously mentioned by several writers under different titles, always unofficial. It was sometimes called *Fantasia* (which is wrong, as a Fantasia is a kind of exhibition cavalry charge) or the *Feast of Sheep* which is just as unsuitable, as this feast is not celebrated in public but by each family at its own home. As for calling it the *Mosque,* this is simply confusing it with another picture from Algiers also belonging to Mr. Biddle. The subject here is perhaps a funeral feast held after the death of a marabout, and the 'Kasbah' is the Arab quarter with white houses and minarets which appears on the left of the picture. The local populace, tiered on the slope of a hill, surrounds in a circle some Arab musicians, dancing and singing to the accompaniment of tambourines.

The whole is inundated with sunlight which dims the shapes of objects. Renoir said of this picture: 'When I gave this picture to Durand-Ruel, it looked like a mere heap of paint. He had confidence in me, and several years later, when the colours had worked themselves in, the picture emerged is I had meant it to look.'

Path climbing through Long Grass

Comiot Bequest, 1926
There is often a human element in Renoir's landscapes; here, women and children are taking a walk along a footpath winding among the tall grass. A brilliant red sunshade provides a gay note of colour in the meadow.

irl with a Straw Hat   Girl seated   Woman in White reading

The Bathers. Painted about 1918
Canvas: 43¹/₄ × 63 in. (110 × 160 cm.) Cat. R.F. 2795

This picture remained in Renoir's studio, at the Villa des Collettes at Cagnes, till his death; it was given by his son to the Nation in 1923, and shown at the Luxembourg; it was put in the Louvre in 1929.

This is the last big canvas which Renoir painted. It was shown at the Salon d'Automne in 1920, and given by his son to the Nation in 1923. This donation was nearly refused owing to the unfavourable comments it aroused. For a long time afterwards, in fact, the bathers, done in Renoir's later manner, shocked bourgeois taste and far more violent deformations of the human body at the hands of contemporary artists were needed to make them acceptable.

We must be especially grateful to the heirs of the artist, Pierre, Jean, and Claude, for having selected this work with which to perpetuate the memory of Renoir in the Louvre, for it is the most important of all his works during the Cagnes period, and in it are concentrated twenty years of research. In his youth, Renoir had painted graceful feminine figures, smiling and ephemeral as those in Watteau's pictures, but from 1900 onwards, or thereabouts, he aimed higher. As Cézanne had done already, he dreamed of reaching that supreme level of painting at which the old masters had excelled—the nude in natural surroundings. But while Cézanne turned towards Poussin, Renoir stems from Rubens. These two figures, who have gone back to a state of pristine innocence and whom he wanted to

call nymphs rather than bathers, are soaking in a kind of primordial mud, a mixture of earth, flowers, grass and stone. The same glowing fluid circulates in their bodies and in those Eden-like meadows. During his Impressionist period Renoir balanced hot colours against cool; during the Cagnes period, he preferred the colour of blood and life, the colour of Rubens: red. One reason, however, why he heightened these reds was to forestall the phenomenon of fading of which they are the victims only too often in painting. He had seen this happen, round about 1900, to his pictures of the Impressionist period. Renoir's foresight was wise. I have known this picture for thirty years, and I have seen it change from lobster-coloured red to a softer lake tone, already beginning to take on reflections of mother-of-pearl.

PAUL CÉZANNE, 1839–1906

Head of an Old Man

Rue Rémy at Auvers

The Repentant Magdalen. Painted about 1866–1868
Canvas: 65 × 49¼ in. (165 × 125 cm.) Cat. R.F. 1952–10

Painted shortly before 1870 on the wall of the salon of the Jas de Bouffan; offered to the Nation in 1907 by Monsieur Granel, who acquired the Jas in 1899 with all the décor of this room, and refused, on the advice of Léonce Bénédite, the curator of the Luxembourg; it appeared at Saint-Germain-en-Laye in the Alphonse Kann collection, then in the Bokanowski collection in Paris; it was bought for 8,000,000 francs by the Louvre in 1952 with funds from an anonymous Canadian donor.

During his first period up to 1870 Cézanne adhered to the Romantic tradition of painting literary, erotic and pathetic subjects in sombre tones and with thick layers of paint. Long despised, this way of painting is only now beginning to find favour with the public — as seen by the adventures of this picture.

It was painted directly onto the wall and later detached and backed with canvas, and was, along with others, in the big drawing room of the house of Cézanne's parents. Cézanne subsequently inherited the Jas de Bouffan, an eighteenth-century folly just over a mile from Aix-en-Provence.

These panels consisted of several experimental works by Cézanne, apparently between 1860 and 1870. Of these, the *Magdalen* is one of the latest.

191

Before being taken down from the wall, it was joined to a *Descent of Christ into Limbo* (in a private collection in Paris) which, in my opinion, was painted somewhat earlier.

The subject of the picture is not certain. She is called the *Magdalen* or *Grief*. She is very similar to the *Melancholy* by Fetti. The effect of Fetti's picture on the *Magdalen* is very obvious and explicable when we remember how often Cézanne took old pictures as models. He may have seen Fetti's *Melancholy* in the Louvre, which he was continually visiting at this time.

In order to conceal the damage to the paint as a result of detaching the picture from the wall, it was covered by a restorer with a veritable make-up of a brown shade. The removal of this has revealed all the violent expression of this work.

A Modern Olympia. Painted about 1873
Canvas: 18 × 21¹/₂ in. (46 × 55.5 cm.) Cat. R.F. 1951–31

This picture was shown at the first Impressionist exhibition in 1874 (No. 43); it was bought from Cézanne by Dr. Gachet; it was in his collection at Auvers-sur-Oise, then passed to his son, Paul, who gave it to the Louvre in 1951.

Cézanne's first manner, lasting till about 1872, was Romantic and sombre; it was inspired by Daumier, Delacroix and Manet, and included

literary subjects *(Temptation of St. Anthony, Judgment of Paris)* and realistic subjects *(Afternoon in Naples, Bacchanal,* etc.) almost all impregnated with a rather forced eroticism.

Among these may be included this *Modern Olympia,* a kind of parody of Manet's *Olympia* (see page 116). Cézanne had painted a first version of it in 1870 in his usual sombre colours. There, hunched up on a bed, a naked courtesan was being admired by a man sitting looking at her. A negress stood in an alcove beside her.

In 1873, at Dr. Gachet's, as a result of an animated discussion (such as often took place between these two violently opinionated persons) on the subject of Manet's *Olympia,* Cézanne immediately started a new version of his *Modern Olympia.* This shows the effect of the painter's new point of view, for only the subject has remained the same. The style has become dazzling. The whole scenario resembles a spirited sketch in the manner of Fragonard. The colours are startling. The negress, with a generous gesture, unveils the woman's nakedness in the midst of a kind of white cloud. A huge bouquet occupies a third of the canvas, a red lacquer stand balances the left side of the picture, while the spectator (Cézanne himself?), boldly drawn with a riding crop and a wide-brimmed hat, looks on. There is also an amusing little dog, sitting on the floor. The whole ensemble, framed on the left by a tall curtain with a tasselled border, is presented exactly as if it were a scene in a theatre.

This *Modern Olympia* is one of the three pictures which Cézanne sent in 1874 to the first Impressionist exhibition on the Boulevard des Capucines. It was very badly received by the public, and scoffed at by the critics.

Still-life with Yellow Dahlia   *Still-life with Green Apples*

Still-life with Accessories

Flowers in a Delft Vase. Signed and painted about 1873
Canvas: 16 × 10¹/₂ in. (41 × 27 cm.) Cat. R.F. 1951–33

In Dr. Gachet's collection at Auvers-sur-Oise; in Paul Gachet's collection; given by Monsieur Paul Gachet to the Louvre in 1951.

Cézanne stayed nearly two years in the Pontoise district. His stay at
Auvers lasted from the end of 1872 to the beginning of 1874. It was one of
the most decisive periods in his career as a painter, and also one of the
happiest in the life of this unstable and nervous individual. He was for a
long time free from tension; this was due in great measure to the soothing
presence, the kindness and tact of Pissarro, and also to the neighbourly
welcome and artistic comprehension afforded by Dr. Gachet.

It was here that Pissarro's advice persuaded Cézanne away from dark
colours to a lighter palette.

His production while at Auvers varies between these two tendencies, and
nothing shows this better than a comparison between this small shining
bouquet and other still-lifes painted at the same period, all in the studio lent
him by Dr. Gachet.

Thus, *Still-life with Accessories* (also called the *Solari Medallion*) (see
page 195) where the plaster-cast and a napkin alone emerge from the shadow, or else the *Still-life with Yellow Dahlia* (see page 194) illumined very
feebly by a few flowers, belong to his sombre, thick, and Romantic manner.
But he soon got tired of these browns and greys, and he began to paint
flowers, which Madame Gachet obligingly picked for him in her garden
and which she arranged in a gaily-coloured, blue-and-white Delft vase.

195

At the same time he painted some *Dahlias* in another larger Delft vase. Here the colours are also bright and gay.

The two Delft vases, the small one seen in this picture, and the larger one, have both been preserved at Auvers, first by Dr. Gachet and then by his son. The latter has been generous enough to include these two precious souvenirs of Cézanne with the collection of pictures which he has donated to the Louvre.

La Maison du Pendu (The House of the Hanged Man). Signed and painted in 1873

Canvas: 21¹/₂ × 26 in. (55 × 66 cm.) Cat. R.F. 1970

This picture was bought by Count Doria at the first Impressionist exhibition in 1874 (No. 42); as a result of persistent requests by Chocquet, Count Doria gave him this picture in exchange for another of Cézanne's, the *Melting Snow* (Chocquet collection); at the Chocquet sale, July 1 to 4, 1899, it was bought by Count de Camondo for 6,510 francs; it was

bequeathed by him to the Louvre in 1908, entered in 1911 and exhibited there in 1914.

The most interesting and beautiful picture of the Auvers period is incontestably *La Maison du Pendu*, in the Louvre. Cézanne's conversion by Pissarro to Impressionism was a very slow process. Most of the landscapes of this period bear witness to his hesitations. Touches with a light brush have not completely ousted the heavy brushstrokes, nor the palette knife, his usual weapon hitherto.

Both techniques can be seen in *La Maison du Pendu*. Traces of colour put on with the palette knife can be found in the sky and on some of the walls. Other parts are more lightly worked over. The complete colour scheme is definitely a bright one. Tone division appears in the foreground In fact this is a key picture. The same thing applies as far as its construction is concerned. The choice of subject suggests a wish to create large masses; those steep roads isolate the house and make it spring out of a hollow.

There is no trace left of the Romantic element in this picture — except for the title. According to Lionello Venturi, 'nobody was ever hanged in that house. One can still see at Auvers,' he says, 'the exact site of this landscape. The thatch has been replaced by tiles, the road has been improved, and the subject is no longer interesting.'

La Maison du Pendu was part of Cézanne's contribution to the Impressionist exhibition of 1874 at Nadar's house. The critics did not spare it any more than they had spared the *Modern Olympia,* and one of them did not hesitate to publish his contempt for the artist in the following words: 'Monsieur Cézanne will excuse us for not coming as far as *La Maison du Pendu.* We prefer to stop on the way.'

The Bridge at Maincy. Painted about 1879
Canvas: 23 1/2 × 28 3/4 in. (58.5 × 73 cm.) Cat. R.F. 1955–20

Sold by Cézanne to 'Father' Tanguy; bought by Chocquet, very probably at the 'Father' Tanguy sale held on June 2, 1894 (No. 10), when it fetched 170 francs under the title of the *Bridge*; the *Hotel Drouot Gazette* of June 19, 1894, mentions the sale, calls the picture the *Bridge at Mennecy;* at the Chocquet sale on July 1 to 4, 1899 (No. 81), entitled the *Little Bridge,* it fetched 2,000 francs and passed into the Molyneux collection, Paris; the Louvre bought it from Monsieur Edmond Molyneux for 30,000,000 francs in 1955.

According to a tradition going back to Chocquet this picture was thought to have been painted at Mennecy near Corbeil (Seine et Oise), where Cézanne stayed in 1897. However, the subject has recently been discovered — still intact — at Maincy, a village near the town of Melun (Seine et Marne), where it is known from his correspondence that Cézanne stayed between June 3, 1879, and February 25, 1880, and later on in 1894. The date 1879 (for the picture was obviously painted in the summer) is quite consistent with the compact brush-strokes which still recall the Auvers

period. Very soon Cézanne's style was to loosen up, becoming round about 1890 like that of a watercolourist.

The *Bridge at Maincy* is transparent, lively, set like a stained-glass window. The shade and the freshness are almost tangible. The stillness is absolute. No breeze disturbs the sleeping stream.

In order to give a stronger impression of form to this landscape of trees, leaves and water, Cézanne has pushed the sky out of the picture, thus banning every cloud from the air and all reflection from the water. He gives to the splendour of the spring foliage the effect of precious stones. The little parallel blobs of paint resemble the facets of cut emeralds. Conforming to custom, the artist has firmly marked in the vertical (the trees on the left) and the horizontal (parapet of the bridge) lines of the composition.

Dr. Gachet's House

Painted at Auvers in 1873. Under the influence of Pissarro, Cézanne's palette became brighter, and his handling of paint less heavy. This evolution is apparent if one compares this picture with the *Maison du pendu,* which must certainly be earlier.

Farmyard at Auvers   *Poplars*

L'Estaque. Painted about 1882–1885
Canvas: 23¹/₄ × 28³/₄ in. (59.5 × 73 cm.) Cat. R.F. 2761

In the Caillebotte collection; bequeathed to the Louvre by Caillebotte in 1894 in the Luxembourg in 1896 and the Louvre in 1929.

Cézanne, who did not care much for conscription, passed the period of the Franco-Prussian war at L'Estaque, an industrial suburb of Marseilles by the sea, where his mother had a small house. He came back several times between 1876 and 1829, and at this time painted out-of-doors. For his friend Chocquet, he did a *Sea at L'Estaque*, but was still feeling his way and the composition is complex. It was only a little later, after 1883 and for about six years (after which he abandoned this part of the coast for the Mont Ste-Victoire) that he found exactly the two subjects which corresponded to what he was looking for.

The first shows, as he wrote to Pissarro 'red roofs on a blue sea'. The view is taken from high up, and plunges down upon the shining roofs of the little town. The sea stretches limitless to the horizon.

The Louvre picture called *L'Estaque* is part of the second subject and is the masterpiece of the series. In the foreground are the hills of L'Estaque with 'olives and pines which never lose their leaves', in the background the chain of mountains, modelled like the facets of a prism against the clear sky, and between these two planes, the calm cerulean spread of the bay. The vertical and the horizontal are well defined, the first by the

201

factory chimney, the second by the strand around the bay. Impressionism looks for movement. Cézanne wants to attain stability. He tries to 'remake a Poussin from Nature.' He remains Impressionist by his fidelity to nature and by employing a single colour to indicate volume; but the light that he paints is the untarnished light of the Mediterranean described in immortal verse by Paul Valéry in the *Cemetery by the Sea,* of which this picture, more than anything else in painting, reminds one. The still sea, like a slab of sheet-iron, pricked out with two white sails, surely invokes 'this calm roof with the marauding seals'.

This is one of the few pictures which Cézanne signed. Traced in red and half effaced, this signature was invisible before cleaning.

The Blue Vase   *Still-life with Fruit Basket*

Still-life with Soup Tureen. Painted about 1883–1885
Canvas: 25¹/₂ × 31⁷/₈ in. (65 × 81 cm.) Cat. R.F. 2818

This still-life belonged to Pissarro, then to Monsieur Auguste Pellerin; according to Monsieur Robert Ray, Monsieur Pellerin bought it directly from Pissarro through Octave Mirbeau, one of Cézanne's admirers from the first moment.

Bequeathed by Monsieur Auguste Pellerin to the Louvre in 1929 with two other still-lifes (see page 203, and page 207).

Apart from oranges, and above all the apples which he has made famous, the accessories used by Cézanne all have this in common: they were never objects of luxury. On this point Cézanne is more austere than Chardin, who always painted the most ordinary objects, but ones not lacking in a certain refinement of shape.

With Cézanne this is never the case. The round jam pots, the plain plates, the pots and jugs of grit stone, ordinary bottles — these are his favourite materials. Everything is sacrificed to volume and shape. The decorated and almost luxuriant soup tureen, which appears in this still-life, is an exception.

The Louvre is fortunate in having, thanks to the generosity of Monsieur

Paul Gachet, some of these 'humble objects' which Cézanne once used as models for his still-lifes: a water jug in grit stone of the ordinary kind then in use, a commonplace kitchen knife and a glass with a stem, amongst other things. They all appear in his well-known pictures, and are all full of memories and hidden life beneath their worn appearance.

The background in these pictures is always furnished; never, or hardly ever, is it neutral in shade. Behind these still-lifes there is always a second still-life: curtains, wallpapers or furniture, serving as decoration to the objects in the foreground. In this picture, it is pictures hanging on the wall. Among them on the left is a landscape, which is thought to be by Pissarro, though there is no proof; it is a road seen in perspective, giving a depth to the background of Cézanne's picture.

The Card Players. Painted about 1885–1890
Canvas: 18 1/2 × 22 in. (47.5 × 57 cm.) Cat. R.F. 1969

In the collection of Ambroise Vollard, Denys Cochin, Durand-Ruel, and Isaac de Camondo; given to the Louvre by Count Isaac de Camondo in 1908, entered in 1911 and exhibited there in 1914.

We know how irritable and shy Cézanne was. He only liked to paint human beings when the sitters were, apart from himself, his wife, who was patient and resigned and posed for him twenty times, a few intimate friends, servants, gardeners, peasants, youths, all humble and respectable people who sat for hours without uttering a word. The sittings were long, so the pose had to be simple. This accounts for all the models who are sitting, hands crossed on their knees, or elbows leaning on a table. *The Card Players* is no exception. The sitters are the ordinary locals. The player on the left is doubtless 'Father' Alexandre, a gardener. Both were separately objects of several studies, head and shoulders, full-face or profile, under different names like *A Peasant, Man with a Pipe, Smoker leaning forward*, etc.

This theme, common in the seventeenth century, but abandoned since, may have come to Cézanne through a picture in the museum at Aix-en-Provence, from the studio of the Le Nain brothers. It was, for Cézanne, a real exercise in composition. He made five versions: one with five people, three players and two spectators; one with four persons, three players and one spectator; and three times, two persons only (Louvre; Courtauld collection, London; private collection in Paris). The two first pictures had a décor as well as their many figures. In both there are hangings and a pipe-rack with four pipes. The first had in addition a dresser, some jugs and a picture, framed on the wall. The cards were spread out on the table.

In the three other versions, which are much barer, not only have the spectators and the third player vanished, but the accessories have gone too. There is nothing to attract the eye but the players. Even the chair of the one on the left is only suggested. On the other hand Cézanne has added to the table a cloth devoid of any cards, and a simple bottle of wine. This last is of very great importance in the picture. The axis of this canvas is carefully composed on the principles of the strictest symmetry.

The Bathers

Apples and Oranges   *Still-life with Onions*

The Woman with a Coffee Pot. Painted about 1890
Canvas: 25¹/₂ × 31⁷/₈ in. (130.5 × 96.5 cm.) Cat. R.F. 1956–13

Bought by Monsieur Auguste Pellerin from Josse Hessel in 1904; in the
Jean-Victor Pellerin collection; given to the Louvre by Monsieur and
Madame Jean-Victor Pellerin, in December 1956 on the occasion of the
fiftieth anniversary of the artists's death.

This picture, as is often the case with Cézanne, raises several problems.
First of all, the date: Cézanne never dated his pictures. Art historians are
therefore not in agreement over the date to be assigned to it. The majority
have, however, decided on a date round about 1890. This means, in the
Cézanne canon, the end of his constructive period, and the climax of his
classical manner.

It is one of Cézanne's most monumental pictures, and one of those in
which he best attained the aim of his researches. 'The Woman with a Coffee
Pot,' says Lionello Venturi, 'gives the impression of an imposing natural
force. The woman is planted there like a strong tower.' Before this human
monument, one naturally thinks of that austere kind of classicism practised
by Piero della Francesca.

Cézanne in these portraits is not interested in the psychological aspect.
He would rather in fact have an insignificant, shy sitter, whose humility
and indifference would not upset his irritable nature. Cézanne only asked
of them absolute stillness, the stillness of still-lifes ('Do apples move?' he
crossly asked a sitter exhausted from holding the pose for a long time.)

The vivid colour of this portrait contributes to its monumental character.

Cézanne 'built' his pictures by means of the richness of his colour.

Two more questions occur to us, looking at this woman. Who was she? Where was this picture painted? Once again no one knows for certain. It is thought that it was done at the Jas de Bouffan, although the setting and the accessories never recurred in the other compositions which Cézanne painted on this family property. The sitter may be one of the servants (cook, laundress?). This is only a supposition. No preparatory work which might help to elucidate these points is known. There is a drawing in an English collection, the head and shoulders of a woman, possibly a preparatory sketch.

PAUL GAUGUIN, 1848–1903

The Alyscamps at Arles. Signed and dated 1888
Canvas: 36 × 28¹/₂ in. (91 × 72 cm.) Cat. R.F. 1938–47

This was one of the thirty canvases sold by Gauguin at the Hôtel Drouot
in February 1891 to raise his fare to Tahiti; it fetched 350 francs.

It was in the collection of Viscount Guy du Cholet; January 10, 1923, Countess Vitaly gave it to the Louvre in memory of her brother, the Viscount du Cholet; it was shown at the Museum of Decorative Arts, where it remained till it was put in the Louvre in 1938.

In 1888 Gauguin gave way to the pressing and friendly urging of Van Gogh and joined him at Arles, where Van Gogh dreamed of creating a 'school of painting of the South', with artists working together as in the seventeenth century. The school was to be directed by Gauguin. They lived together for two months, during which time Gauguin influenced the art of Van Gogh to some extent and Van Gogh revealed Japanese art to Gauguin. But their two temperaments clashed. Incessant arguments got on their nerves, and the episode finished tragically when Van Gogh, in a moment of madness, nearly killed Gauguin.

Gauguin's style is seen to have developed in this view of the Alyscamps. The colour is warmer, even intense, as is shown by that flamboyant red patch of a bush, beside a blue fir tree, among the yellow foliage of October. This landscape is far removed from the objectivity of Impressionism. It tends to be stylised. One feels that Gauguin is now ready to create a style of his own, which was indeed the case, during his visits to Brittany soon afterwards.

In this view, Gauguin has placed himself outside the cemetery, which he depicted with more precision in his *Alley of the Alyscamps at Arles*. The ruins of the chapel of St-Honorat rising up behind a clump of trees is visible, however.

Van Gogh painted four versions of the Alyscamps at the same time. The best known is in the Kröller-Müller Museum at Otterlo.

La Belle Angèle. Signed and dated 1889
Canvas: 36¹/₄ × 28¹/₂ in. (92 × 72 cm.) Cat. r.f. 2617

This portrait was offered by Gauguin to Madame Satre who refused it; it was one of thirty canvases sold in 1891 by Gauguin at the Hôtel Drouot (No. 3) to pay for his journey to Tahiti; it was bought at this sale by Degas for 450 francs; then bought at the sale after Degas' death in 1918 (No. 42) by Ambroise Vollard for 3,200 francs.

Given to the Louvre by Ambroise Vollard in 1927; at the Luxembourg

from 1927 to 1929 when it was transferred to the Louvre.

In the spring of 1889, Gauguin left the inn at Pont-Aven where he had already stayed several times, chased away by the influx of tourists. He went to Pouldu and settled at the inn, Le Gloanec. Before he left, he wanted to leave a souvenir for the innkeeper's worthy wife, Angèle Satre, whose husband was about to become mayor of Pont-Aven. She gave Charles Chassé later on her recollections of Gauguin: 'He was very gentle and very poor, and we liked him a lot. But at that date his painting frightened us a bit.' Gauguin began her portrait. 'While he was working at it he would never let me see the picture, and always covered it up at the end of each sitting.' The sitter later said that 'other painters to whom Gauguin showed his work laughed at it.' Madame Satre, knowing this, became biased against it in advance. Fearing a scandal she exclaimed: 'How frightful!' when Gauguin, 'very pleased with himself, came to offer her the picture which she refused. Gauguin was very upset and said, in disappointment, that he had never succeeded so well with any portrait as with this one.'

Degas agreed with Gauguin for he considered this picture a masterpiece. He acquired it at the sale Gauguin held in 1891 and kept it till his death.

This stylised image powerfully expresses the spirit of synthetism and symbolism with which the primitive Bretons inspired Gauguin.

This picture has been called one of the first characteristic works to show a Primitivist feeling, but it has not been noticed that the pose is taken from a much earlier masterpiece in the Louvre: Holbein's *Anne of Cleves,* which had inspired Degas thirty years before (see page 133).

The Seine at the Pont d'Iéna

The Red Dog

Still-life with Guitar　　　　　　　*The Schuffenecker Family*

Women of Tahiti. Signed and dated 1891
Canvas: 27 × 35¹/₂ in. (69 × 90 cm.) Cat. R.F. 2765

In Viscount Guy du Cholet's collection; given by him to the Louvre in 1923; first shown at the Luxembourg, and then, in 1929, at the Louvre.

On June 8, 1891, Gauguin, wishing to escape from Paris, from poverty and the stupidity of the public, disembarked at Papeete, the capital of the island of Tahiti, a French colony. Finding the town too full of Europeans, he buried himself in the country about twenty-five miles away to the south, and lived like the natives, choosing from among them a mistress, Tehoura. He started work with zest and in 1892 wrote to his wife, who had remained in Denmark: 'I have eleven months of finished work, forty-four worthwhile canvases, which makes at least 15,000 francs for the year, provided my clients buy.' But they did not, and Gauguin had to return penniless.

After a period of adaptation, the nature life began to thrill him: 'I am pleased with my work,' he wrote to his wife, 'and I feel I am getting to know the character of these dwellers in Oceania. I am certain that what I am doing has never been done by anyone, and that nothing like it is known in France.

Women of Tahiti, also called *On the Beach,* belongs to a series painted

213

in 1891, the first year of his stay in Tahiti. The pictures of this first visit are still fairly objective; later on he sought a more poetical interpretation with symbolic features (*White Horse,* see page 216, and *Vaïrumati,* see page 217). Gauguin accentuated the squat bodies of his sitters and made them even fatter, if one can judge by the wrist and neck joints, in order to accentuate their primitive character. The individual on the left is shown in an attitude very often used by Gauguin: all the weight of the body rests on the outstretched arm with the hand on the ground. Although the bodies keep their volume, the décor is reduced to several superimposed planes.

The pose of these two women is found in different versions of the picture dating from 1891 and 1892.

214

Breton Landscape. The Mill

From the Matsukata Collection
    This landscape, painted on his return from Tahiti, is very different from those he had done earlier at Pont-Aven and Pouldu. It is saturated in colour, in shades of flame and gold; Gauguin sees the grey Breton countryside with eyes dazzled by tropical sunlight.

The White Horse. Signed and dated 1898
Canvas: 55$^1/_2$ × 36 in. (141 × 91 cm.) Cat. R.F. 2616

    In the collection of Georges Daniel de Monfreid, the painter-friend of Gauguin; acquired from Monsieur de Monfreid for 200,000 francs by the Louvre in 1927 shown at the Luxembourg, and at the Louvre in 1932. Monsieur de Monfreid gave the Louvre, on the occasion of this sale, the manuscript of *Noa-Noa* written by Gauguin in 1893–94 with Charles Morice, recalling his first voyage to Tahiti, and illustrated by Gauguin with some delightful watercolours.

    This is one of the most mysterious paintings of the second period in Tahiti. Gauguin himself explains (and this applies to the whole of the work of his second stay in Tahiti) that he wants a luxuriant nature, with its unkempt brushwood and shady streams, to convey the idea of the mystery of Tahiti. Hence the brilliant colours, the burning air, strained and silent, and he talks of the 'difficulty of expressing all these heights and depths on a canvas of about one square yard!' This explains why he has to crowd together, and even superimpose, the different planes, as in some of the primitives. Gauguin refuses to paint depth, which he considers deceptive, like a *trompe l'œil*. His decorative instinct is here given full play, and his gift of rhythm makes one regret that he was never asked to decorate some great public halls, as for instance was Puvis de Chavannes (whom Gauguin appreciated).

    The nude horseman high up on the right reappears in a picture also dated

1898 *(Faa Iheihe)* in the Tate Gallery, London.

When Daniel de Monfreid gave up the *White Horse*, which he was anxious to see in the French National Museums and for which he had refused a far bigger price from a Munich art lover, he kept a copy of this picture which he had painted himself in 1911. This copy was shown in 1938 at the Charpentier Gallery.

Vaïrumati. Signed and dated 1897
Canvas: 28³/₈ × 36⁵/₈ in. (72 × 93 cm.) Cat. R.F. 1959—5

This picture was sent by Gauguin on December 8, 1898, to Vollard the
dealer; it was in the Matsukata collection at Kobe, Japan, and became

French property by the terms of the peace treaty with Japan. Allotted to the Louvre in 1959.

Gauguin returned to Tahiti in July 1895. He fled from Papeete, which he considered too Europeanised, and settled on the west coast of the island where he had a large Tahitian-style hut built for himself.

A year later, he was ill and suffered horribly. Loneliness weighed upon him and he gave way to moments of despair. He wrote to Daniel de Monfreid: 'I feel so demoralised and discouraged that I can't imagine how things can get worse.' But as soon as he felt better he began to work; 'I am getting better and I have taken advantage of it to get through a lot of work.'

He painted this picture in 1897. In *Noa-Noa* Gauguin painted the story of Vaïrumati as told to him by Tehoura, his Tahitian wife: 'She was tall and the sun's fire burnt in the gold of her flesh, while all the mysteries of love slept in the night of her hair.'

This figure is, therefore, no longer a model posing, as in *Women of Tahiti* (page 214), but a person taken out of a legend. We meet her again on the left-hand side of the triptych: *'Whence come we, what are we, where are we going?'* She is sitting in the same pose in the foreground, and beside her is a pelican holding a lizard, or rather, as Gauguin explained in a letter to Daniel de Monfreid in February 1898, 'a strange white bird holding in its claws a lizard, representing the uselessness of vain words.'

Behind, on the right, are sitting two nude women one of whom is carrying a goblet of fruit in a gesture recalling the *Redflowered Breasts*.

In Gauguin's Tahitian work there are more nudes than landscapes. These figures are motionless and in appearance always calm, with thoughtful expressions. To accentuate this immobility, the persons represented are sitting, lying, or leaning against the ground. The women are massive, with thick limbs. Gauguin in *Before and After* describes them: 'What distinguishes the Tahitian woman from all other women, and often causes her to be mistaken for a man, is the proportions of her body. Nude, she is Diana the huntress with wide shoulders and narrow pelvis ... the skin is a golden yellow.'

The Gold of their Bodies

Breton Village in the Snow
Canvas: 25¹/₂ × 35¹/₂ in. (65 × 90 cm.) Cat. R.F. 1952–29

Acquired by Victor Ségalen at the sale in Papeete in 1903 of Gauguin's hut at Atuana (La Dominique) after the artists death; it was bought for 7 francs together with four panels carved by Gauguin for his hut, which fetched 16 francs; acquired for 9,000,000 francs by the Louvre in 1952, with the panels of the hut and a palette from Madame Joly-Ségalen, out of funds from an anonymous Canadian source.

According to Victor Ségalen, the only person to see Gauguin's hut, this picture was standing on an easel there. At the enforced sale of Gauguin's effects at Papeete, it was shown upside down and christened the *Niagara Falls* amid the laughter of the audience.

This landscape has been considered Gauguin's last work, in which he was thinking of the hoar frost of Europe before dying in the tropics. But in my opinion the truth is otherwise. Gauguin only painted from nature or a model. This picture, however, presents close analogies with others, painted in Brittany at Pont-Aven or Pouldu, either in 1888 or during Gauguin's visit on his return from Tahiti in the November and December of 1894. I would rather settle for this last date because there were several heavy snow-falls in November and December 1894 in Brittany.

Arsène Alexandre said Gauguin took two Breton landscape with him. Letters from Gauguin to Vollard prove Gauguin had some Brittany pictures with him in Tahiti. In the letter Victor Ségalen wrote to Daniel de Monfreid from Papeete, he said he had purchased 'two studies done in Brittany.' They were both mentioned in his memorandum of purchases at the sale; one called the *Niagara Falls*, the other the *Oxen* (it shows peasants leading oxen through the snow past a stone Calvary). In the *Mercure de France*, 1904, Victor Ségalen speaks of the pictures in the Louvre as 'the work of his last moments, *reworked in those bright lands*'.

Victor Ségalen, rummaging in his memory, later helped to spread the legend. What is probable is that Gauguin retouched this picture at Atuana.

ODILON REDON, 1840–1916

Wild Flowers in a Long-necked Vase. Signed and painted after 1912
Pastel: 28³/₈ × 20⁷/₈ in. (72.5 × 53.5 cm.) Cat. R.F. 30 570

In the Marius-Ary Leblond collection; given by the Society of Friends of
the Louvre in 1954.

Afer 1900 flowers were the main feature of Redon's work. The subjects were always small or large bunches, arranged in vases of all shapes and sizes, always placed on an imaginary plane in the centre of the canvas, against a unified background which was either light or dark, and generally with no accessories to distract the eye. These *Wild Flowers* are made up, as in most of his bunches, of real flowers idealised by the imagination of the artist, for Redon's studies were a mixture of observation and fantasy.

In this pastel in the Louvre a blue, vertical branch of larkspur is noticeable, also some brilliant poppies, opening out in a long pedestal vase. The technique employed during the previous years (1912–16) is ample and solid, with strokes in pure colour and so widely spread on the canvas that they no longer give a glittering impression, due to hatching and separated brush strokes, as in his 1905 work.

The poet Francis Jammes, who published an essay on 'Odilon Redon, botanist' in his *Verse and Prose,* thus described his studio: 'We went to the studio, that is to say into a garden, because, oh! wonder of wonders, I have never seen flowers like that. Although painted by the hand of man, even their scent was described! But no one has ever described Odilon Redon's flower pictures so well as he has himself: 'My flowers issue from the confluence of two streams, representation and memory,' he said, 'this is the very ground of art, the good ground of all that is real, harrowed and worked over by the soul.'

Portrait of Gauguin   *Flowers*   *Madame Odilon Redon*

HENRI ROUSSEAU, 1844–1910

The Snake Charmer. Signed and dated 1907
Canvas: 65³/₄ × 74⁴/₈ in. (167 × 189 cm.) Cat. R.F. 37–7

Left in his will to the Louvre by Monsieur Jacques Doucet; given by Madame Jacques Doucet in 1936; shown at the Louvre in 1937.

This picture had been offered by the Douanier Rousseau to the painter Albert Marquet in 1907 for 400 francs.

Rousseau belonged to the Impressionist epoch. Not only because of the time in which he lived, but also by inclination. He was not discovered by Guillaume Apollinaire, Alfred Jarry and the Cubists, as has been asserted. To exhibit at the Salon des Indépendants as soon as its opening allowed self-taught painters to show their paces, was to be labelled a Symbolist by the critics and writers of the *Mercure de France*. In his escapism, his inspiration from dreams, his reduction of a picture to a decorative surface, Rousseau is connected with Gauguin.

It is above all in his large compositions evoking exotic countries that Rousseau's relationship with Symbolism becomes apparent. He claimed that his memories inspired him. He related how, when between eighteen and twenty-three years old, being then in the regimental band, he took part in the expedition which Napoleon III sent out to Mexico to help the Emperor Maximilian. Guillaume Apollinaire recalled this journey in a poem dedicated to Rousseau. His works are in fact the product of pure imagination. As Maximilien Gautier has pointed out, the journey was fictitious.

The variations of critical opinion with regard to this artist can be summed up in these two appreciations by Tabarant, who in 1937 had said of Rousseau, 'his glory has long since touched the heights,' forgetting that at the exhibition of 1912 he had written: 'It was a most successful joke. One wonders if this exhibition is only a farce, or if there really exist people so peculiar as to take it seriously.'

Rousseau put the *Snake Charmer* and *War* (see page 224) among his chief works. In the letters he wrote to the judge to prove he was a great artist, at the time of the trial in 1907 in which his frankness had implicated him, he quoted these two pictures.

War

VINCENT VAN GOGH, 1853–1890

The Restaurant de la Sirène. Painted about 1887–1888
Canvas: 21 × 26 in. (54 × 66 cm.) Cat. R.F. 2325

Madame J. Van Gogh-Bonger's collection, Amsterdam; A. Schuffenecker, Clamart; Joseph Reinach; bequeathed by Joseph Reinach to the Louvre in 1921; shown at the Luxembourg; exhibited at the Louvre in 1929.

Van Gogh's first years as a painter were spent in Holland and Belgium. He painted in a sombre manner connected with the schools of his country.

225

His subjects were rustic landscapes and peasant scenes. But attracted to Paris by his brother Théo, and also under the influence of some inner compulsion which caused him to go farther and farther south towards the sun, he arrived there in 1886 and stayed two years. At Goupil's, where Théo worked, he met Degas, Monet, Sisley and especially Pissarro, who had shown himself friendly and helpful towards Cézanne in 1872 and towards Gauguin in 1883. Van Gogh followed his advice, started separating his tones, and strokes, and above all lightening his palette. From now on he ceased to paint 'black'. He saw works by Rembrandt and Delacroix in the Louvre, admired the Japanese prints and discovered Monticelli for whose art he developed a cult. In Paris, he led an exciting life which he enjoyed but which overstimulated his irritable temperament.

He painted a great deal, mainly landscapes and still-lifes. *La Guinguette (The Tea Garden)* (see page 228) was one of the first pictures he painted out-of-doors, in Montmartre. In it can be seen the transition from the Dutch manner to *peinture claire* (i. e. painting the dark tones after the light and half-tones). The drawing of the street lamp, the alcove and tables is brown and thick, but they are seen against a clear sky, and the atmosphere is airy and luminous. *The Restaurant de la Sirène,* painted a year later (1887), shows how rapid was the development of Van Gogh's ideas. He definitely abandoned all social preoccupations. He discovered Impressionism, the techniques and subjects of which he completely adopted. This picture recalls the work of Monet and Sisley.

Vincent's Room at Arles. Painted in 1889
Canvas: 22½ × 29 in. (56 × 74 cm.) Cat. r.f. 1959–2

In Werner Dücker's collection at Düsseldorf in Paul Rosenberg's art gallery in Paris; it belonged to Prince Matsukata, Kobe, Japan; became French property in 1952 by the terms of the peace treaty with Japan. Allotted to the Louvre in 1959.

After passing two years in Paris and changing his style, Van Gogh became more sensitive than ever to the call of the light. He selected Arles. He hoped to find there landscapes like Japan, about which he continually dreamed, the landscapes of Monticelli and Cézanne, and the sun.

At the beginning of his stay he was happy. The climate and the purity
of the sky enchanted him. 'Here I see everything in a new way.' His first
work was calm and serene *(The Pont de l'Anglois,* Amsterdam Museum;
Trees in Blossom). But an extremely gruelling bout of work, with long
periods of sitting in the burning sun, and the mistral, were bad for his
ultra-nervous temperament. When, in October of the same year (1888),
Gauguin, whom he begged to join him, did so, Van Gogh, in an attack of

227

madness, tried to kill him, then to punish himself cut off a piece of his own left ear *(Self-portrait with a Bandaged Ear,* Leigh Block collection, Chicago). This is the room Van Gogh was living in at the time of the drama. The first version of this picture was made in October 1888 (Chicago Art Institute) before Gauguin arrived. The version in the Louvre, as well as another (V.W. van Gogh collection, Laren) were done by Van Gogh from memory, while he was under treatment at the hospital at St-Rémy. The dimensions differ somewhat from the first picture, but all the rest is the same. 'I have been greatly entertained doing this interior from nothing,' he wrote to his brother, '. . . in flat tones but thickly brushed up into a full impasto. The colour should impart, by its simplification, a grander style to things It should suggest sleep and rest. To look at this picture should rest one's brain and one's imagination . . . The shadows are suppressed. It is coloured in flat, frank tones, like Japanese crepons.'

This picture, with all its furniture and other accessories well arranged round a huge empty surface, and with no human being present, is really only an immense still-life.

Van Gogh only lived in this room for a few months. His nervous attacks grew worse, and he was admitted to the asylum where he stayed for a year.

The Tea Garden   *Head of a Peasant Woman*

Fritillaries   *Portrait of the Painter Boch*

Dr. Gachet's Garden. Painted in 1890
Canvas: 29 × 32 in. (73 × 51 cm.) Cat. R.F. 1954–15

Given by Van Gogh to Dr. Gachet; in Paul Gachet's collection and given by him to the Louvre in 1954.

At the beginning of his stay at Auvers, calmed by Dr. Gachet with whom he found himself in immediate sympathy, Van Gogh began to paint furiously, with the approval of, and indeed urged by, the doctor, who thought that work would be the best distraction for the invalid. 'Come and work up at my house whenever you like,' was the welcome invitation from the doctor, just as he had invited Cézanne eighteen years earlier. In fact Van Gogh felt, at the doctor's house, as if he were at home. It is curious, therefore, that he never painted nor drew the doctor's house, as Cézanne did over and over again (see page 200). He did, however, decorate the dining room and paint the garden. *Dr. Gachet's Garden* is mentioned in a letter to Théo (June 4, 1890): 'I have painted two studies at his place, which I gave to him last week, an aloe with marigolds and cypresses, and last Sunday white roses, vines, and a white figure walking among them.' This last study also went to the Louvre, in the Paul Gachet donation (see page 232). The 'white figure' is the silhouette of Mademoiselle Gachet, the doctor's daughter, whom Van Gogh painted on another occasion playing the piano (Basle Museum). The first study mentioned in the letter is the

229

Garden from the Louvre. Dr. Gachet's garden is one of the first pictures painted at Auvers—in fact, during the week of his arrival. If the exact date were not known, it could easily pass for a corner of the Provençal countryside near St-Rémy. The name 'cypresses' in the letter proves that Van Gogh was haunted by the vegetation of the South. Behind the yucca, to whose pointed leaves the sharp drawing of Van Gogh has given the menacing aspect of daggers, stands a yew tree, painted as if it were a cypress at Arles, a huge flame rising and bending its branches beneath a cobalt-coloured Mediterranean sky.

Portrait of Dr. Gachet. Painted in 1890
Canvas: 26³/₄ × 22¹/₂ in. (68 × 57 cm.) Cat. R.F. 1949–16

Dr. Gachet's collection, at Auvers-sur-Oise given to the Louvre in 1949 by Mademoiselle Marguerite and Monsieur Paul Gachet.

Van Gogh, on leaving the asylum at St-Rémy, was sent by his brother to Dr. Gachet at Auvers-sur-Oise, for Dr. Gachet was interested in mental cases. On his arrival, Van Gogh, who considered the doctor eccentric, described him thus in a letter to his brother: 'Dr. Gachet's house is full of old-fashioned dark things, except for his Impressionist pictures. I hope I shall stay on with him and paint his portrait.' On June 4 he wrote: 'I am working on his portrait. On his head, which is very blonde and fair, is a white hat. I have given him a blue frock coat against a cobalt blue background, and he leans against a red table on which a yellow book and a purple-leaved digitalis plant are placed. Monsieur Gachet is quite mad about this picture and wants me to paint one for him, if I can, exactly like this one.' In a letter to Gauguin: 'I have now done a portrait of Dr. Gachet wearing the distressed expression typical of our times.'

Van Gogh first of all made an etching of the doctor, then the two portraits quoted. The first shows two books, *Germinie Lacerteux* and *Manette Salomon*. In the second the sitter holds a branch of digitalis (symbol of specialisation in heart disease) and the books are not there. Paul Gachet says that these two works show 'a changing frame of mind within a very short time together with a singularly unstable state of health, superficially scarcely noticeable, but appearing in his work, though much simplified by his brush. Here he is impetuous, carried away (in the first version), there, less nervy, in the grip of a minute attention to detail, *which was possible for him for a very short period.*'

The doctor's hat is among the souvenirs given to the Louvre by his son.

Caravans   *Mlle. Gachet in the Garden at Auvers*

Roses and Anemones   *Two Peasant Girls*

Self-portrait. Painted about 1889
Canvas: 25¹/₂ × 21 in. (65 × 54 cm.) Cat. R.F. 1949–17

Dr. Gachet's collection at Auvers-sur-Oise; given by Mademoiselle Marguerite and Monsieur Paul Gachet to the Louvre in 1949.

Van Gogh was at first happy in the asylum in St-Rémy (May 1889 to May 1890). He was looked after by understanding doctors and had a good deal of freedom. He could paint, and even had a studio, but the harrowing crises of anguish and madness recurred with disturbing regularity. During the intervals between them, he painted—views of the asylum, landscapes in the open air or seen from his window, flowers, portraits of his doctors and keepers, or of himself, pictures inspired by the work of other artists (Rembrandt, Daumier, Gauguin and above all Millet for whom he felt a boundless admiration). But these respites were haunted by the fear of future crises which he knew to be inevitable, and this anxiety affected his painting which became more and more over-excited. He became the victim of an obsession for the sun, painting colossal revolving suns. The fields take on an appearance of arabesques, the cypresses are twisted by the heat and resemble great sombre flames. It is towards the close of the year 1889, at St-Rémy, that one can probably date this *Self-portrait.* There is some controversy on this point, some critics placing it later, during a short stay in Paris, or on his arrival at Auvers in May 1890. The reasons put forward are based on letters from Van Gogh to his brother Théo, describing all the pictures he was painting. But his self-portraits are too numerous, and the details too

indefinite, for it always to be possible to differentiate them. Whether it was painted at St-Rémy or six months later in the Paris region, this portrait, sometimes called *Vincent in the Flames,* shows no trace of the nervous tension shown in many of the works of the Auvers period. It proves how hard Van Gogh concentrated on dominating his madness, until the final collapse. It is a supreme balancing feat, on a summit, but beside an abyss.

234

Painting can never go any farther. This is without doubt the artist's masterpiece.

This portrait was copied in pastel by Mademoiselle Blanche Derousse
(Cabinet des Dessins, Louvre) and also by a Japanese artist.

Cottages at Cordeville. Painted in 1890
Canvas: 28¹/₂ × 36 in. (72 × 91 cm.) Cat. r.f. 1956–14

In Dr. Gachet's collection given by Monsieur Paul Gachet to the Louvre
in 1954.

'Auvers ... has a grave beauty. It is in the heart of the countryside,
which is characteristic and picturesque.' 'There are many old thatched
cottages, which are becoming rare.' Thus Van Gogh expressed his joy at
discovering the little village of Auvers, simple and rustic with its grey and
brown roofs, and its humble houses which have attracted so many painters,
as I showed in an exhibition held in 1954. Corot, Daubigny, Pissarro,
Cézanne, had evoked its peaceful charm. Van Gogh transformed it into a
volcanic territory, the houses of which seem twisted by a tempest. Van Gogh
became a demon for work there, and painted unceasingly as if he knew
that his days were numbered, more than seventy pictures in two months!

This picture is one of the 'two studies of houses surrounded by greenery'
of which Van Gogh speaks in a letter to his brother on June 10, 1890.
The other is in the museum at Toledo, U.S.A. He painted numerous views
of the village with its steep streets, its crooked cottages, half ruined, and
whose picturesque appearance suited the agitated texture of his style.
Perhaps however the little simple, rustic houses reminded him of his native
village. A picture painted at St-Rémy in March 1890 to evoke Holland
for him is, though wilder, very much like this one. This picture shows
stability in its construction, with its houses well propped up in the hollow
of a hill, and a lay-out of superimposed step-terraces in the sun. But this
effect is in contrast to the dishevelled, tormented drawing which causes
the roof to go in waves, forms the branches of the tree in spirals bigger
than itself, transforms into arabesques the menacing accumulation of
clouds, inflates the road in the foreground, changes the little field into a
green waterfall and gives the whole scene an aspect of fantasy.

This picture was known as *Cottages at Montcel;* Monsieur Paul Gachet, when he gave it to the Louvre, corrected its name. The district shown here is not Montcel, but Cordeville, which is another part of Auvers.

The Church at Auvers. Painted in 1890
Canvas: 37 × 29 in. (94 × 74 cm.) Cat. R.F. 1951–42

In Dr. Gachet's collection at Auvers; acquired for the Louvre in 1951, by agreement with Monsieur Paul Gachet.

The most expressive of all Van Gogh's paintings of Auvers-sur-Oise and its countryside is undoubtedly this view of the church. It had remained

unknown until it reached the Louvre in 1951, and was a revelation for everyone all over the world.

Like most of the villages of the Ile de France near Paris, Auvers-sur-Oise has a fine thirteenth-century church. Its simple yet elegant lines are part of what one might call that classic serenity which is a quality of early Gothic art. Set solidly on the ground, it is, as it were, the token expression of the solidity of the peasants who worship in it. As seen by Van Gogh, it appears as if uprooted by an earthquake. All its lines are wobbling and the classic thirteenth-century church has become a monument of the Flamboyant period. The two paths look like two rivers of mud. The intense, almost black, Prussian blue of the sky is a colour divorced from reality, and imparts a strange nocturnal depth to the picture.

It was between June 4 and 8, 1890, that Van Gogh, writing a letter to his sister, Wilhelmine, described this picture: 'I have done a bigger picture of the village church, an effect showing the building purple against a simple, deep blue sky of pure cobalt. The stained-glass windows appear as patches of ultramarine blue, the roof is violet and partly orange. In the foreground there is some grass with flowers and some sand, rose-coloured with the sun on it. It is almost the same thing that I did at Nuenen (1884–85) of the old tower and the cemetery, but in the present picture the colour is more expressive, more rich.'

Van Gogh only painted the church at Auvers once. It appears only in the distance in the general views of the village, notably in Daubigny's *House and Garden at Auvers,* which he painted several times and which he mentions in his letters of June 17 and July 23, 1890 (V. W. van Gogh collection, Laren). In this last letter he draws a sketch of this view.

GEORGES SEURAT, 1859–1891

Port-en-Bessin. The Outer Harbour, High Tide. Painted in 1888
Canvas: 26 × 32 in. (66 × 81 cm.) Cat. r.f. 1952–1

Shown at the Salon des Indépendants in 1890; bought by Monsieur Paul Alexis at the Seurat sale; later bought by Monsieur Garibaldi of Marseilles; bought from his son in 1923 by Monsieur Alfred Lombard; sold to Monsieur Paul Rosenberg in 1951, and bought from him for 16,742,349 francs by the Louvre in the same year, out of funds from an anonymous Canadian donor.

The work of Seurat, which is very scarce owing to his early death and the enormous labour which his method of painting entailed, comprises three

kinds of pictures. These are: the 'little sketches', very small as a rule (see below), painted from nature in a spontaneous Impressionist technique; some twenty landscapes done in pointillist technique, probably begun out-of-doors and finished in the studio; finally some pictures painted in the studio.

The *Port-en-Bessin* in the Louvre shows signs of quite large brush-strokes beneath the layer of pointillist colour, as if the artist had first of all covered the canvas, using the same technique as he employed for his sketches, and had later applied some small strokes to this ground work. This explains why the white canvas is not visible between the circular strokes of his brush.

The pointillist border painted on the edges of the canvas with great finesse was done by Seurat himself. Speaking of the borders of two views of Le Crotoy, Félix Fénéon says: 'These two (landscapes) are enclosed in a border painted on the canvas itself; such an arrangement prevents those shadow areas which a frame gives, and allows the frame to be coloured to fit the picture.' This frame is theoretically blue, because only the complementary colours emitted by the bordering colours show up. 'To these normal reactions, Monsieur Seurat added another element; the blue or the orange according to whether the light fell on the landscape from the back towards the front or the other way round; one can only praise him for having given up those practices which were admissible before the existence of a frame.'

Seurat's sea pictures give out a kind of scintillating luminosity; the landscape seems to give out light rather than receive it. Charles Angrand said of the artist: 'He is the first to express the feeling of the sea on a calm day.'

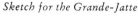

Sketch for the Grande-Jatte   *Sketch for the Grande-Jatte*

  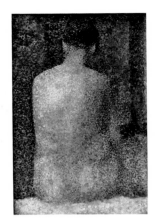

Model in Profile   *Standing Model*   *Model from the Back*

The Circus. Painted in 1891
Canvas: 70⁷/₈ × 58¹/₄ in. (180 × 148 cm.) Cat. R.F. 2511

It was shown at the Salon des Indépendants of 1891; in the collection of Paul Signac; then in the collection of John Quinn (No. 123 in the catalogue of his collection published by the Pidgeon Hill Press, Huntington, U.S.A.); given by Quinn, who died in 1925, to the Louvre where it was shown in 1927; also shown at the Luxembourg.

The circus has often attracted painters. Seurat, though, aimed to discover the laws of the absolute through the mask of appearances; the calm promenades of a *Summer Sunday at the Grande Jatte* suited his temperament better. Later, however, he approached the more difficult problem of pinning down movement on to canvas, his attempts resulting in such pictures as *The Circus*, the *Chahut* and the *Parade*.

The picture in the Louvre was painted after the artist had spent long evenings at the Cirque Médrano. From the variety of different acts he chose the equestrienne, also painted by Lautrec. The colour in this painting is a little unrewarding, because the picture is not finished, although Seurat showed it in this condition at the Salon des Indépendants in 1891. Unfortunately his death, from an infectious form of angina contracted at the very moment when he was arranging the Salon, prevented him finishing it.

The frame painted round the edge of the picture, as well as the large surround in wood coloured in pointillist style, are not by Seurat. Félix Fénéon informs us that after the death of the artist, surrounds of this

241

nature, which alter the harmonies of the picture, were added. In my opinion, they are easy to distinguish from those made by Seurat himself, not only because of the difference in pictorial quality, but by the poor technique.

HENRI DE TOULOUSE-LAUTREC, 1864–1901

Jane Avril Dancing. Signed and painted about 1892
Cardboard: 33¹/₂ × 17³/₄ in. (85 × 45 cm.) Cat. R.F. 37–37

In the Personnaz collection; given to the Louvre in 1935.
At Degas' suggestion, Toulouse-Lautrec studied and painted dancers. But

they did not frequent the same society. Degas went to see the dancers at the Opera. He painted the ballerinas on stage, or in the practice-room. Lautrec found his models at the Moulin Rouge and in the night clubs. Degas' dancers are always anonymous. It is their gestures not their faces that interest him. Lautrec's portraits are very different. Whether it be Loié Fuller, La Goulue, Jane Avril, they are given their names, they are good likenesses, they preserve their personalities. This portrait of *Jane Avril Dancing*, painted in 1892, was done in one evening at the Moulin Rouge. The Moulin Rouge, celebrated *café-concert* opened on October 5, 1889, was the pleasure centre of Paris. Its opening was an 'event,' and its success immediate. Foreigners from every country hurried there, and mixed with the Parisians. Jane Avril was one of the leading lights. She was the natural daughter of an Italian nobleman and a courtesan. After obscure beginnings, she made a sensation dancing under the name of La Mélinite. The very original choreography of her number enchanted Toulouse-Lautrec. 'In the middle of the crowd,' so Paul Leclercq, a friend of Lautrec, tells us, 'there was a sudden eddying movement and the people closed up round a central figure, which was Jane Avril dancing. She turned to and fro, graceful, light on her feet, a trifle mad, pale, thin thoroughbred . . . turning back and forth, light as a feather, flower-fed. Lautrec was loud in his admiration.' The figures she executed were always sideways; she always danced alone; she enhanced her different steps by harmonious costumes and appropriate colours. Her orange, black or lilac dresses were famous for their refined elegance. Her grace and distinction, poles apart from the vulgarity of La Goulue, fascinated Lautrec. He was even more attracted by her face, 'pale, nervous, ailing,' her intelligence, and also by a quality of bitter sadness. Endowed with some degree of culture, she was worthy of a better setting. Like himself she seemed abandoned. A strong mutual sympathy brought them together. She believed in Lautrec's value, and was always delighted to pose for him. For two years he painted her many times: dancing, arriving at the Moulin Rouge, leaving it, putting on her gloves, in the street, from the back, from the front.

Justine Dieuhl

Portrait of Honorine P.

Cha-U-Kao, the Female Clown. Signed and dated 1895
Cardboard: 25¹/₄ × 19¹/₄ in. (64 × 49 cm.) Cat. R.F. 2027

Bought by Count Isaac de Camondo from Toulouse-Lautrec for 5,000 francs, and bequeathed by him to the Louvre in 1908; put into the collection in 1911 and exhibited in 1914.

According to Ambroise Vollard, Camondo did not dare put it with the other pictures in his collection but hung it in his dressing-room.

This female clown with the Chinese name appeared at the Moulin Rouge and Lautrec took her likeness on many occasions. The one in the Louvre is one of the finest and most penetrating. It was done during his most fruitful period. The influence of Degas can still be felt, but the colour is more intense: bright blue costume, plain yellow collar, thrown into relief by the red of the sofa and the green background of the wall. This portrait is powerfully composed, with a magnificent scroll encircling the woman, the start of a spiral of yellow tulle beginning at the bottom of the picture on the left, and ending at the very top of the picture in the white tufted wig which prolongs the effect. The locale is apparently a private room in a restaurant, for the edge of a white napkin is visible, and a cloth on the corner of

245

a table, while above, a mirror reflects the figure of an old man in evening dress.

A large full length portrait of this female clown is in the Oskar Reinhart collection at Winterthur. Another half length, with hands in pockets, is in the William Powell Jones collection in America. A third, very well known, shows her in the same costume, sitting facing the artist, her legs apart in a somewhat provocative pose, while on the left are seen some masked persons waiting for the procession to start. The museum at Albi owns a large drawing in Chinese ink, showing the procession on the same gala-evening, with Cha-U-Kao making her entry astride a donkey, and surrounded by a sham policeman, sham firemen etc., while in the audience, in the background, the outlines are visible of Toulouse-Lautrec and his 'shadow,' his cousin and friend, Dr. Tapié de Celeyran. Other sketches and studies were made preparatory to all these compositions, and also as preliminaries for posters advertising the Moulin Rouge.

Panel for La Goulue's Booth. Signed and dated 1895
Canvas: 117³/₈ × 122 in. (298 × 310 cm.) Cat. r.f. 2826

These panels were bought in 1900 from La Goulue by Dr. Viau, who was a great admirer of Lautrec and Degas; they were in the Viau sale on February 21, 1907, and were bought by Druet for 5,200 francs; after a period in a collection in Scandinavia, the two canvases were bought by Hodebert, who, in 1926, cut them up into eight large pieces and countless small ones; they were bought by the Louvre in 1929 and repaired; they were shown at the Luxembourg, and at the Louvre in 1947.

La Goulue, or Louise Weber (her real name), left her job as a laundress to act in the Cirque Médrano. She used to frequent the Moulin de la Galette. Then she appeared at the Jardin de Paris and at the Moulin Rouge in 1890. She remained its 'star' for five years.

Lautrec never got tired of watching La Goulue and her partners and drew them in hundreds of posters, lithographs, and paintings.

But her success came to an end. La Goulue, who owed her nickname to an insatiable appetite, was getting fat. She installed herself in a booth at the Foire du Trône, where she appeared in Egyptian costume dancing the belly dance. It was then, in 1895, that she asked Toulouse-Lautrec to decorate her booth, which he did in two panels.

Lautrec, in the left panel (see page 248) wanted to show the dancer's past. The scene is the Moulin Rouge. In the foreground the disjointed outline of Valentin the Boneless, beginning to do the 'splits.' Near him is La

Goulue doing her old number. They are surrounded by the habitués of the Moulin Rouge.

The other panel shows the present, namely the dance of an oriental nature which La Goulue was offering just then. She is wearing light gauze and spangles, and holds the stage, while behind her the ladies of the harem provide local colour. In the middle of the foreground is Jane Avril in black and wearing her big hat; close up against her, the outline of Lautrec himself, wearing a bowler; on the extreme right, the sharp satanic profile of the critic Fénéon; towards the left of the panel, the gross shape of Oscar Wilde; on his left, Dr. Tapié de Celeyran; at the piano at the back Sescau, the photographer.

La Goulue's end was a sad one. She became an animal tamer, a wrestler, and a flower-seller. She sank into poverty and alcoholism, and died in 1929.

Woman with a Black Feather Boa

Woman putting on her Stocking

Panel for La Goulue's Booth (Detail)

Woman in front of a Bed

The Bed

Portrait of Madame Lucy

The sitter is shown three-quarter back view; but the face is in profile, turned to the right. Concentrating on essentials, and executed on grey board, this work is more of a drawing than a painting.

La Toilette

Woman combing her Hair

Portrait of Paul Leclercq

The sitter was a friend of Lautrec, and wrote a book of reminiscences about him *(Autour de Toulouse-Lautrec)*. He was astonished that the artist could have completed his portrait in only two or three hours; and this is indeed more than a little surprising, since the work is not executed in the style of a sketch.

Portrait of Louis Bouglé

Toulouse-Lautrec was a close friend of this enthusiastic sportsman, known in cycling circles as 'Spoke', and painted several portraits of him. This picture shows him sitting fishing on the parapet of the quay at Arromanches, in May 1898.

LIST OF ILLUSTRATIONS

The page numbers in italics refer to colour plates.

254

258

INDEX OF NAMES

261